THEY CALLED HER CASSANDRA

THEY CALLED HER CASSANDRA

A Story of Survival

Renée Tyack

Book Guild Publishing
Sussex, England

First published in Great Britain in 2008 by
The Book Guild Ltd,
Pavilion View
19 New Road
Brighton, BN1 1UF

Typesetting in Times by
TJO Typesetters, Prenton, Wirral

Printed in Great Britain by
CPI Antony Rowe

A catalogue record for this book is available from
The British Library.

ISBN 978 1 84624 269 4

For

Stefan, Julie, Joe, Silas, Sebastian

With Love

'Live well, it is the greatest revenge …'

From *The Talmud*

Contents

Acknowledgements

My grateful thanks to:

My writers' group
    Caroline Natzler, Caroline Gallup and Barbara Rennie, for their positive and professional guidance through four drafts of this book.

Gertrud Nolterieke
    For giving her time so generously to translate Ruth's book, Fred's letters and Third Reich documents.

Jessica Lack and her writers' group
    For persuading me that the story should go beyond the family.

Maggie Prince
    For her professional advice and encouragement.

My family and friends
    For their patience in listening, and reading excerpts.

Tim Huggins
    For his valuable feedback.

My brother Tom

For his wonderful memory, for our visit to Leipzig, for all his love and support throughout this project.

Ronald Harwood

For providing another memory of Ruth and Fred and writing such a moving Foreword.

Foreword

In 1952, I was a student at the Royal Academy of Dramatic Art. One of the other hopefuls in my year was an attractive, bubbly brunette with lively dark eyes. We became friends, student friends, a comradeship born of shared interests and daily contact in class. Our rapport, I now suppose, may also have been encouraged by the fact that we were the only two Jews in the place. However, my friendship with her was to prove important, at least for me. In truth, my friendship with Renée Tyack, née Brent, turned out to be a life-saver.

A little personal background is, I'm afraid, necessary. I had arrived in England from Cape Town where I was born. My parents were both emigrants from the pogroms in Lithuania and Poland that drove the Jews to far-flung lands at the end of the nineteenth century. I grew up with a driving ambition to be an actor and so it was thought I should try my luck in London. By the time I left Cape Town my mother was widowed and working to support her family. Somehow, she raised the necessary funds to send me on my way, pay the fees at RADA and give me a small living allowance. I was always broke and often looking for cheaper and cheaper digs. It didn't seem to bother me much. I lived from day to day, optimism rampant, 'in case', as Mr Micawber says, 'anything turned up'.

The Brents turned up. Neither Renée nor I can now remember the precise details but, because I suspect I was as usual almost penniless with nowhere to stay, I found myself at the home of Renée's parents, Ruth and Fred Brent, 74 Overton Drive, Wanstead, where I was to stay the night in a warm, comfortable bed. I recall an extremely enjoyable evening and being asked lots of questions about my background and present circumstances. But what I remember most, and remember vividly, was standing at the bus-stop the next morning, checking to see if I had enough money for the fare. I felt something unfamiliar in my pocket. It rustled and crackled. Eager to discover what it was, I withdrew my hand and found I was clutching one of those bygone, large, white five pound notes. A fortune. A great fortune. I knew instantly who was responsible for this anonymous, magnificent windfall. My luck had changed.

More than 50 years have passed but I have never forgotten, and never will forget, that wondrous act of generosity. Then, out of the blue, towards the end of 2007, Renée sent me her book, her loving and fascinating memoir of her parents, and asked me to write an introduction. What I set down is an entirely inadequate way of expressing my gratitude to Fred and Ruth.

To my shame I knew little about my benefactors. I remembered that Fred was a doctor. I knew Ruth was an active Zionist because the only time I had met Renée in the intervening years was when I was invited to give a talk at a lunch arranged by Ruth for her women's Zionist group; but of the family's extraordinary history, their hair-raising escape from Nazi Europe, their making of a new life in England, nothing.

Contained within the pages that follow is Renée's beautifully written account of her parents and their triumph in rebuilding their lives which had been shattered by the Nazis. Because Renée's memories are so personal and peppered with extraordinary details, this is not just another tale of refugees and the Holocaust. It is a portrait of two remarkable human beings whose strength and values of decency, tolerance and kindness were unshaken by the terrible events that threatened to obliterate them, as it did so many others. This book is a monument to goodness.

Ronald Harwood
London, 2007

Prologue

'It was a gentleman's agreement! You can't go back on that! I insist you do as we all agreed!' My mother banged her fist on the table. Our Sunday lunch quivered in the dishes and the cutlery rattled. I sat, head bowed, intent on the thin winter sunshine filtering through the French windows making patterns on the yellow tablecloth. My father, mid mouthful, stopped chewing. Would he understand what I had done? My brother fidgeted uneasily intent on a rapid escape to his room. Never one to restrain her emotions in the secure, small circle of our family, to the outside world my mother was invariably serene, smiling, charming. 'I'm fine,' was her automatic response to all enquiries, no matter how great her pain or how ill she was. On this occasion she had no hesitation in venting her full rage on me. We were discussing my forthcoming marriage and I had just announced, with some trepidation, that I was going to break a part of our 'agreement'.

My fiancé was Polish. He had happily agreed to a number of conditions: that he become a British citizen; that he should not take me back to Poland (this was hardly likely as he would face almost certain death at the hands of the Communist regime if he returned); and most important, that he change his name. It was this last condition that I alone had defied. I didn't feel it was right to say, 'I'll marry you but only after you change your name.' Especially as Szendzikowski was an old and respected name in Warsaw.

So why this passionate attack from my mother? At the time I did understand her reasons, but was much too involved in my own emotions to sympathise with her. Later, in calmer moments, I acknowledged her fear, but never regretted my stand in taking my husband's Polish name, incurring weeks of frosty silence from my mother.

Why was she so afraid?

In 1946 we had changed our name from Bergmann to Brent, the most bland, inconspicuous name to be found in the telephone directory, in order to disappear into the vast ocean of 'Englishness'. Now, ten years later, I was about to assume a foreign name, which would make me different, easily identifiable, potentially threatened. Her fear for me was real, arising from the horror of their last years in Germany. Having saved our lives she wanted no hint of danger to touch us again.

It is this story of our escape that she urged me to tell, 'Lest we forget'. A story repeated many times to my brother Tommy and me, as we grew, and later to our children. I wish I had listened more carefully and asked the questions that haunt me now. But, as a child I was frightened by the raw emotions – sorrow, anger, hate – hard as she tried to control them, and later I was embarrassed.

A tale of survival, pieced together from various sources: the documents from Germany; our father Fred's letters from internment in Liverpool and then on the Isle of Man, and those he wrote everyday to our mother, Ruth, as a locum in 1946–47; the books she wrote for Tommy and me, recording our progress and changing circumstances from our birth; and finally the taped conversation I had with my father when he was an old man and remembered so much.

The Quakers, who were instrumental to our escape, had persuaded her to write the events of our last months in Leipzig, as they considered it important for this experience to be set down. There are, tragically, many, many stories of that time, brave and sad. But the situation of a surgeon operating under house arrest in the Jewish hospital right up to the end of August 1939 was, they felt, unique. Ruth followed their advice and filled several note-books, initially in German, then in English. She kept them in an old cardboard box. Unfortunately, a domestic help she had in Wanstead during the late 1950s thought they were rubbish and threw them away. A desperate chase to the depot was too late, so my mother's record was lost. She didn't have the heart to start again. So she passed the baton on to me.

Sometimes my brain aches with the effort of remembering and my heart aches, remembering. The people we live with, the people we love, we accept from childhood onwards like a warm blanket; they are always there like gentle background music, not closely observed or analysed. It is only when there is a joyful or discordant note, a clanging, that we wake from our slumber, take note, remember. Sometimes moments of happiness, often moments of conflict. I hope this memoir of two brave and loving people who created a little dynasty here in the UK and in the USA is as complete and balanced a portrait as possible.

1

Fred

Leipzig, Germany – Spring 1938

The young surgeon is completing his last ward round of the day, accompanied by an increasingly nervous sister as they approach an empty bed.

'Where is Herr Gruber?' he asks.

'They took him and his wife this afternoon.'

'They! What do you mean "they"?' But of course he knows.

'The Gestapo.' The nurse's voice shakes. 'They said there was nothing wrong with him or his wife. That they could go home. You know I couldn't stop them!'

The surgeon's pallor reflects his white coat. The Gestapo are right, of course, there isn't anything medically wrong with the old couple, and they are not the first he's put in a bed to save them from concentration camp or deportation. He understands what 'home' means. Herr and Frau Gruber are Polish Jews. They will be deported back to a hostile Poland with nothing but the clothes they have on their backs. But they are both over 60 years, over the age limit to be sent to the camps or for deportation, a ruling mostly ignored by zealous Nazis. There is still a chance...

'Do you know where they took them?'

'Herr Gruber said they'd be taken to the station and to tell you thank you for what you did for them and...'

But he is already at the end of the ward and taking the stairs two at a time. The street outside is quiet, peaceful, the trees swelling with early foliage. He runs, turning left and left again into the main road.

'Taxi! Taxi!' The shabby black cab draws up.

'The station. Hurry!'

In the gathering dusk the lights illuminate the scene. Under the great latticed dome of the station he finds the platform, a seething sea of humanity, some openly weeping, others trying to look brave as they say goodbye, clutching the few possessions they have been allowed to take with them. Police and railway officials are everywhere, checking lists, pushing people onto the train, slamming doors shut. The black-booted Gestapo stand back, watching, some holding dogs on their leashes. At regular intervals the train hisses out a cloud of steam, for a moment drowning out the sounds of misery.

The surgeon pushes his way through the crowd to the edge of the platform. He approaches a policeman at an open door of the train who is striking off names on his list.

'Excuse me. I'm looking for an old couple. They've been snatched from my hospital, out of their beds. They're too old to travel. I have to find them.'

The policeman looks at this young man with an impossible mission. How can he hope to find anyone in this milling human chaos?

'What's the name?' he asks.

'Gruber.'

The policeman's finger moves slowly, page by page down his list. He reaches 'G'.

'You're in luck. They're here!'

His white coat flapping, the surgeon runs up and down the train, brushing people aside and shouting: 'Herr Gruber! Herr Gruber!' The policeman follows, opens doors, echoing the name carriage by carriage. A face appears at a window, confused, afraid.

'That's him! That's him!' shouts the surgeon. 'Herr Gruber, get out! Where's your wife? Get her out! Quickly!'

The two old people stumble out of the carriage, uncomprehending, grasping both the surgeon's hands.

'Thank you! Thank you!'

'Get them out of here!' grunts the policeman, turning his back and hurrying away up the platform.

Herr and Frau Gruber are safe … for the moment.

The young surgeon is my father, Fred Bergmann.

*   *   *

He was born, in 1907, Walter Manfred Bergmann, always to be known as Fred. He came from humble beginnings: his grandfather, Lazarus, bought and sold farm animals while his grandmother, Sara, looked after their five children, four boys and a girl. They lived in a primitive house with grilled apertures at ground level where the cattle were kept. They had no running water. Jews were not allowed to own land, so the prospects of progression in rural life were limited.

The next generation were determined to better themselves. Fred's father and uncle established a small department store on Eisenbahnstrasse in east Leipzig, Kaufhaus Gebruder Bergmann. The first two floors were the business, 'a dry goods store' as my grandmother called it, selling clothes, linens and other household effects. The two brothers married two sisters and they lived above the store. My grandparents, David and Thekla, lived on the third floor. When the children arrived they had cousins on hand to play with. The premises were on a prime site at the junction of two main streets, with trams criss-crossing into town and the suburbs. The building itself had no electricity when the family moved there in 1910. Fred remembered with pride how his father built a generator in the back yard with an accumulator in the shop basement, so they were able to have a lit sign above the store – very avant garde – and rent electricity to the neighbours. The family also let out two to three flats on each floor, mostly to non-Jews, as well as having their own apartments. So Fred was born and brought up, with his younger sister, Erica, in an integrated, working-class environment. His father kept the fast on Yom Kippur but seldom went to the synagogue, and Fred's attendance there in his teens was, by his own admission, 'the best way to meet the girls'. His boyhood friends were the sons of the butcher opposite and all the children played in the courtyard, but were strictly not allowed in the store.

During the Great War the family were fortunate in having relatives in the country who could supply them with enough fresh food, unlike Ruth's family who suffered considerable deprivation. Her lifelong ill health was probably due to starvation in her growing years; she regularly collapsed in the street on her way to school.

Fred studied medicine at the University of Vienna and at the university in the picturesque medieval town of Freiburg, but it was while he was still in his last term at school at the Schiller Gymnasium in 1926 that he met Ruth. They were both billed to perform in a concert at a club. Ruth was looking for someone to accompany her on the piano. Fred played the saxophone and clarinet in a band, but on this occasion he was to play four hands on the piano with his sister, Erica. Ruth's older sister, Leni, who was organising the event, negotiated with Fred to accompany Ruth. For him it was love at first sight, but Ruth was involved with another young man, Rudi, for whom she still held affectionate memories many years later. Leni's comment after the concert, 'He has very nice eyes' may have had some effect because they soon became inseparable. Her parents nicknamed him 'grunspatz' (the green one) referring to his seemingly permanent student status and his youth; they didn't think he had much to offer in the way of security for their daughter. Fred was tempted to go into the family business so they could marry quickly, but Ruth, seeing his potential (and perhaps preferring the title of Frau Doktor rather than just Frau!), insisted he continue with his medical studies, and they were engaged for seven years.

The relationship lasted for 67 years. They were esteemed by all as a devoted couple, always together unless circumstances such as internment forced them apart. And they were well matched, their opposing natures achieving a successful balance: Ruth with her intuition and strength in her beliefs, and Fred, often beset with doubts, trusting to the point of naïvety, able to see both sides of an argument. It was his trust that 'things will get better … this will blow over' that delayed our departure from Germany; a trust reinforced by a relative easing of repression during 1936–37 when the world's scrutiny was on the Olympic games in Berlin. He felt himself to be a German citizen. His upbringing gave him a sense of security. Also, he was gaining a reputation as a fine surgeon, earning good money, but it was Ruth's instinct for survival and her energy that saved our lives. A fact he never let us forget, characteristically omitting any mention of his own heroic deeds.

Ruth and Fred were married on 20 July 1933. They spent their wedding night with the band at a pre-booked gig out of town.

Perhaps to celebrate, perhaps because they'd all had a bit to drink, they decided to continue the session after the official engagement had ended. In a sleepy little town square, a band lustily belts out the latest Duke Ellington. The police are called, by the irate, local residents and if one of the band who, unbeknown to the rest, was a member of the Nazi party, hadn't used his influence, they would have spent the last few hours of their wedding night in jail!

1933 was also the year that Hitler came to power, thus accelerating the repressive legislation against the Jews in Germany. '*Juden Verboten*' became a familiar sign in parks, stores, restaurants, cinemas and other places of entertainment. The fear and encroachment upon normal life are hard to imagine. For Fred this manifested itself in a number of ways. He had two great passions as a young man. He loved football. He played outside right in first the youth team, then the second team for a famous club, VFD. They were German champions, and he was well known as a talented player in Leipzig. He remained an ardent supporter of Manchester United until the end of his life. His other passion was jazz. His band played at weddings, parties and gigs, travelling around the country in a bus, with girlfriends in attendance, including Ruth, of course! The money he made in the band helped to pay his university fees. Both club and band, most apologetically, asked Fred to leave. 'Just temporarily, old man …this won't last long.' No one was brave enough to refuse to sack a talented footballer and musician, as well as a long-time friend.

Fred loved children and had always wanted to specialise in paediatrics. In 1933 a special decree was announced limiting the number of Jewish doctors and dentists allowed to study and practise medicine. The quota for paediatricians was full, that door was now closed. He was in his mid-twenties, married, with

10

responsibilities, and time was precious in the circumstances. It so happened that the Jewish hospital was desperate for surgeons and when the chief, Dr Ludwig Frankenthall, heard of the young doctor's predicament he immediately sought him out, offered him a job and a crash apprenticeship in surgery. Fred had no choice but to accept, but with some doubts as to his suitability.

At the first few operations he observed he passed out! Things got so bad that Ruth would accompany him so that she could drag him out of the viewing room and help him recover. Observing an operation did not have the same effect on her, quite the opposite in fact. She found the experience fascinating and her expert observational skills were to pay life-saving dividends in the future. From this inauspicious beginning he became an outstanding surgeon. In England during the war leading surgeons at the Manchester Infirmary would send him their most complicated cases or call on him for advice as his reputation grew.

There were so many facets to his personality. He was a good-looking man, slim and energetic. He never walked up stairs, always ran. He had an unconscious charm and a mischievous sense of humour, often directed at Ruth, who rose to the bait regularly and delightedly. On the occasion of their wedding anniversaries he would always ask us children for condolences and then congratulations on making it for another year. After one of their quarrels he gave her The Ink Spots' record 'Ain't Misbehaving'. Another time it was 'Coax Me A Little' by Dinah Shore.

And their romance flickered on. She adored camping and, up to the time when she became too ill, on a fine summer's night they would take a sleeping bag into the garden and spend the night under the stars.

In time he would become a much-loved and respected general practitioner. There must be scores of adults, born and raised in the

East End of London, who remember the doctor with the habit of taking the soft flesh of both their cheeks between thumb and forefinger and jiggling them back and forth. His grandchildren certainly remember. Eyes would water, tiny ones would howl, but all came back for more, understanding that this was his way of showing his affection. As my children grew in strength they would get in first and grab his cheeks and he would laugh with pleasure at the joke. When he retired queues of people wanting to wish him well formed outside the surgery.

Every time I hear a saxophone I think of him and wish that I could have heard him play. Tommy and I often asked why he'd given it up. He'd explain that it was too expensive, they couldn't afford luxuries like that and then he'd lost his ability and it was too late to start again and so on. But I believe now that they had an aversion to anything that reminded them of their life in Germany. I was very intolerant of this attitude, as I grew up, insensitive to their sensitivities. They'd had a large library in Leipzig, they both collected books from childhood. 'Why don't you buy books?' I would upbraid my mother as she struggled with her five books a fortnight from the library. 'You know why!' she would retort. 'We lost our library. I'm not starting again!' They bought Tommy and me books but not one for themselves.

Fred was creative in many ways. In Germany he painted fabrics for Ruth, which she made into dresses. She liked to be unique if at all possible. His ingenuity in making furniture out of nothing made us feel at home wherever we were. I remember a standard lamp made out of four thick slices of tree trunk for the base, broom handles, and a smaller, thinner slice in the middle for a cup or ashtray. Although we missed out on the saxophone and clarinet, we did have an old piano, bought for me to learn, and he would play the current favourites and I would sing along. I still have, nearly 50 years on, a battered, much-travelled biscuit tin with faded apples, pears and cherries painted for me. And the greatest treasure, found when we were clearing the loft in the old house, is his shabby old medical case, bringing back all the memories of Fred rushing out of the house to visit patients. I remember the night of the great smog. They were quite frequent in those winters of the late forties and early fifties but this was one of the worst, a lethal mixture of dense fog and heavy smoke. My father was on weekend duty for eight local doctors and the visibility was so bad that I had to accompany him on his visits, frequently having to walk in front of the car with a torch and a white rag to guide him. On our return to the house I looked at him and burst out laughing.

'Daddy, you should see your face, you look like you've been down a mine!'

'Have a good look at your own!' he retorted.

Once we were settled and secure in Wanstead he turned all his creativity to his garden, which became his greatest interest and escape from the sometimes turbulent household.

My father was 92 when he died on the first of April in the new millennium. It was later that I realised the significance of the date. We had moved to Wanstead exactly 51 years earlier on 1 April 1949, and there our new life began.

Apart from a stroke in his eighties he was remarkably healthy for his age. He was very proud that he had all his own teeth. After his stroke my mother insisted that he use a stick wherever he went to avoid falling. Out of her sight he dispensed with it and confided to me that he was practising falling deliberately because getting up was the tricky part and he was perfecting his technique.

'Don't tell Mummy will you,' he said, with that characteristic wry 'naughty schoolboy' grin.

The last six years of my father's life were fraught with anxiety, anger and frustration. When my mother died in 1993, I welcomed the opportunity to build a closer relationship with him. I always loved, admired and respected him, and to the end sought his approval, but I was never as close to him as I was to my mother. His infatuation with the woman who nursed Ruth in the final weeks of her life eventually drove a wedge between him and his family. She took advantage of his loneliness and age, both financially and, far worse, by attempting to turn him against us and isolating him from any social contacts he had. It was only when she saw that he was deteriorating – and as a nurse she recognised the signs – that she deserted him. However, during those years we did not give up on him. My regular visits to Wanstead continued as did Tommy's from the USA, and Fred's grandchildren saw him as often as time allowed. But it was not a happy experience as we were viewed with a mixture of distrust and guilt, and treated with a lack of affection.

I regret that I did not succeed in breaking down some of the inhibitions between us. To me he remained a figure of authority, a concept perhaps engendered more by Ruth than by him, following the traditions of her own upbringing. And yet it was my father who understood me best; many times he tried to explain my side of an argument, thus incurring my mother's wrath. Perhaps my expectations were not realistic. As I have said, the last few years of his life were stolen from me. However, as a family, we did have seven months at the end: the nurse having deserted him when she realised he was ill, we were able to regain his trust and convince him of our love. And maybe it was not in his nature to show his deeper feelings. He was a shy, extremely modest and lonely man.

2

Ruth

I think it's true to say that my mother has been the strongest influence in my life and though she has been gone for over 15 years, in many ways she still is. When I leaf through her box of hand-written recipes to bake one of her cakes, I feel happy because I know she would be pleased. When I lose my temper (not so often now) I feel her disapprobation.

From when I was a child and well into my thirties the fear of her dying made me feel physically sick, the thought was unbearable. I never thought about my father dying, to me he was immortal. There was a song in the forties, Sophie Tucker singing 'My Yiddish Momma'. I wept every time I heard it, and still do when I hear it now.

I didn't really understand the nightmare my parents faced during the thirties in Nazi Germany until I became a parent myself. To be two adults alone in such circumstances was dangerous; to be responsible for the well-being and the life of young children must have been a constant terror.

My brother, Tommy, was born in our apartment, Sedanstrasse 17a, a block in an affluent part of the city, only a few minutes' walk from the hospital where Fred worked. I was three and have only vague memories of the event, but the smell of the new baby has stayed with me: a subtle mixture of fresh skin, soft downy scalp and talcum powder. And the early intimation of responsibility, someone to look after and protect, eventually to bully and play with.

What must it have been like for her having a second child in the Third Reich in 1937? How much trepidation was mixed with her joy when she first held him? And I think it was brave to give me a brother in the circumstances.

*   *   *

Her friends called her 'Cassandra' because of her persistent warnings of impending disaster, after the coming of the Third Reich. Yet neither she nor anyone else could have foreseen the true horror. She never felt completely at ease in Germany, unlike my father whose (misguided) optimism was grounded in an integrated childhood. Ruth's horizons had stretched beyond national boundaries. Influenced by her father perhaps, she had an early understanding of and empathy for English and Russian literature, and her best friends at school were émigrés from Russia, after the revolution.

'They were all so beautiful,' she would tell me. 'With romantic names straight from Tolstoy – Natasha, Sonya, Tania.'

She was a woman of many complexities and contradictions: strong when threatened, courageous in the face of danger, yet so vulnerable; dominating, yet so insecure; shy, lacking in self-confidence; stubborn and inhibited to the point of prudishness. She was always sure that she was right and almost invariably she was in her intuition about people and situations.

A woman of her time, her potential was thwarted and her expectations limited. She wanted to become an actress. In fact she

16

must have had considerable ability as one of the leading actresses in Berlin offered to take her on as her protégée. She was sent to Berlin, I believe, to complete her education. Here, she was introduced by the composer Kurt Weill (her future brother-in-law's brother) to some of the best creative talent of that time, such as Bertold Brecht. The former had been part of the family from the time Ruth was fifteen when, in 1920, her elder sister Leni had met and become engaged to Kurt's younger brother Fritz. Kurt must have had some feelings for Ruth, manifested many years later. In 1946 the much heralded American musical, *Annie Get Your Gun* – the first since before the war – arrived in London. We were living in a run-down Edwardian semi in Kilburn; the aspects I remember most clearly were the roof felt used as flooring and the furniture made by my resourceful father out of orange boxes with dried milk tins for legs and all painted a tasteful black. Suddenly a letter arrived from Hollywood. Kurt would like to escort my mother to the first night of *Annie*.

At that time my father was studying to retake all his medical qualifications in English, in a single year. Ruth worked as a cleaner, sewed bags for sale and we took in lodgers (one of them turned out to be a notorious murderer on the run but that's for another episode!) and we lived off those earnings. What should she wear? She had no problem in choosing … she didn't have anything. I was sent all over London to every acquaintance we knew to borrow dress, gloves, shoes and bag. Her underwear was her own. But Ruth did go to the ball! Kurt came to pick her up and I thought she looked quite beautiful as she drove off in the elegant black car. Kurt Weill had his pick of glamorous women to accompany him to the much publicised first night. He chose to take my mother. I was never sure how much she enjoyed that evening and how much being thrown into such a different environment was an ordeal for her, but I do know she was immensely flattered. And it left me with a vivid impression of her time in Berlin in the twenties, before she met and married my father.

Ruth was born in 1905, in Markgrafenstrasse 10, a large elegant nineteenth-century town house in the smart centre of Leipzig. The youngest of six children – four girls, and two boys who both died in infancy – she had a close relationship with her sisters whom she adored. The third sister Edith was diagnosed as being 'slow'. Nowadays she would be treated for thyroid imbalance but at the time no such accurate diagnosis or medication was available. And so as children, and until she left home in 1933 to get married, the youngest sister was assigned to look after her and chaperone her everywhere, a task the young, vivacious and flirtatious Ruth found somewhat onerous. In 1939 Edith disappeared and was never heard of again. Ruth feared that she was one of those rounded up in the street and taken to the gassing vans, the first small experiments for the Nazi's 'final solution'.

Ruth's father, Albert, was a tall, elegant man with a moustache and a predilection for English suits and English breakfasts. He had aspirations to be a doctor and had just started his studies when his father died and he became responsible for his sisters. In order to make a living he went into the textile industry where he eventually met my grandmother, Antonia. By the time Ruth was born he was well established, converting three of the twelve large rooms in their luxury first-floor apartment into a gentlemen's tailoring outfitters (hence the preference for Saville Row suits). Leni's daughter, my cousin Hannelore, has fond memories of riding up and down the very ornate, open, wrought iron lift as a child.

My grandfather fought for the Kaiser in the Great War and

considered himself and his family as respectable and loyal German citizens. The intimation that his youngest daughter wanted to go on the stage was akin to her wanting to go on the streets. Her father's threats were enough to discourage her. This was an age when the majority of women had little or no power and certainly no financial independence. She loved and respected her father and the thought of causing him pain was probably enough of a deterrent. But the bitterness of a wasted talent remained. He was a man of his time, with firmly held attitudes on the role of women in society; not a bad father but perhaps an unimaginative man. When I, in my turn, expressed a wish to pursue a career on the stage my mother was delighted. A selfless woman, she encouraged me wholeheartedly and was sincerely thrilled with any success I had.

Forbidden to pursue her chosen career, Ruth launched into a series of jobs, which demonstrated her resourcefulness, her 'chutzpah' and her organisational and management skills. To quote my father, in his eighties and in a voice full of admiration, perhaps tinged with a little awe: 'She was very clever.'

She started as a shop assistant in a large department store, Kaufhaus Gebruder (brothers) Held. Within weeks she was in charge of the children's department and then promoted to running the women's department. After meeting my father at the concert in 1926 (she was 21, he 19), her course changed, maybe influenced by his entry into medical school. She saw an advertisement for a laboratory assistant to a well-known Hungarian scientist who specialised in skin disease and venereal disease. Ruth applied (herein lies the 'chutzpah'!), then hurried to her general practitioner brother-in-law, Fritz Weill, now married to her sister Leni, and asked him for a crash course and any advice he could give relevant to the situation vacant. When she went for the interview she found that she was up against stiff competition, the waiting-room was full of hopeful young women. When her turn came she was asked if she could type. 'No, but I can learn,' was her reply. Her lack of practical experience was obvious, but she got through the interview. As she left, walking through the crowded room and down the stairs, she felt embarrassed at her attempt to join the scientific fraternity. The next day she received a phone call. She'd got the job.

She did learn to type, on the job. She also learnt to dissect guinea pigs and other technical work in the research undertaken, invaluable experience for what lay ahead. The public side of the practice was to treat venereal disease, and later my mother would tell me, with a certain mischievous glee, of the rich and famous who passed through those doors.

This employment came to an unjust end for Ruth. The scientist had begun an affair (conducted on the surgery premises) with one of his patients. When his wife found out, she was convinced that Ruth was 'the other woman' and insisted that her husband sack her, forthwith. Which he did, thus protecting the identity of his mistress. However, he dedicated one of his publications to Ruth, perhaps to show his appreciation of her, perhaps by way of apology.

In an effort to remain in this field, she worked briefly as assistant to Fritz but this was cut short when he started to make advances and she hastily left and returned to the Held store. From there she eventually came to work for my paternal grandfather in his store until she got married.

There emerges an image of a young woman who attracted men on a personal and physical level. She was not beautiful, or even pretty in a conventional sense. She was small, 5 foot 3, and had a life-long struggle with a tendency to plumpness. But her large

20

brown eyes, thick auburn hair, charm, energy and *joie de vivre* made her irresistible. She was a keen cyclist and the test for her many would-be boyfriends was that they had to join her in long strenuous cycle rides before she would go out with them. And most of them did!

Ruth's mother, Toni, was as short as her husband was tall and she was almost as wide as she was short! She had a beautiful singing voice and in another time might well have been an opera singer. As with many women in the social scene of that time, her life revolved around domestic details, servants, entertaining, weekly visits to the theatre, opera and concerts. Leipzig had its own prestigious opera house and a rich cultural life. Traditional festivals and regular visits to the synagogue were observed although they were not a religious family. Ruth and her sisters would invade the kitchen on fasting days and sneak off with provisions, and the synagogue was seen as a social occasion more than a religious one.

Ruth was a wonderful mother and home-maker. Whenever she could she hid her worries from us children and we had a warm, loving and often fun-filled childhood. She wanted the best for us and the best from us. It was these high standards and expectations, often unforgiving, and not uncommon in refugee and immigrant families who are striving for success and ambitious for their children in a new country, that caused such friction between us and has left me with bitter regrets.

3

A Dangerous Situation

Anti-Semitism did not emerge in Germany with the rise of Hitler. It can be traced back to Lutheran times. As detailed in Peter Wiener's book *Martin Luther, Hitler's Spiritual Ancestor*, Martin Luther had his own seven laws, at least as severe as Hitler's, for the expulsion and destruction of the Jews. '*The Jews have to be expelled from the country.*' '*The Jews deserve to be hanged on gallows seven times higher than ordinary thieves.*' His sermons to his followers are spattered with lewd, vicious statements exhorting his followers to violence. '*The Jews are malignant snakes and imps.*'

In the early twentieth century, Jews were not allowed to own land, discouraged and often forced from living in rural areas, and they were concentrated in towns and cities. Many of them were doctors, lawyers, scientists, academicians and, like my grandfather, small business men, as well as all those successful in the arts. The resentment against the Jews was given further nourishment by the humiliating loss of the war in 1918 followed by the punitive Versailles Treaty. Returning soldiers, brutalised by their time in the trenches, unemployed, rootless and missing the order and camaraderie of their wartime experience, volunteered for groups like the Freikorps and Erhardt Brigade, fertile ground for the young army corporal Adolph Hitler to work on by 1920. They were eager to beat up the Bolsheviks, a conveniently broad definition to cover communists, socialists and Jews. The violence was often accompanied by marching songs:

Wir sind kein Judenknechte,
In Deutschland soll immer nur gans allein
Ein Deutscher unser Fuhere sein.
(We are no slave of the Jews,
Forever and ever in Germany
Only a German should our leader be.)

How confusing this must have been to teenagers like Ruth and Fred, who considered themselves to be German.

As they became adults my parents' attitude reflected the Jewish community's dilemma. Fred, ever the optimist, always believing that better times were coming and Ruth, the forewarner, chilled by the rule of terror, by the routine attacks on Jews, hearing the Nazi storm troopers in September 1931 singing:

Crush the skulls of the Jewish pack,
And then the future is ours and won.
Proud waves the flag in the wind,
When swords with Jewish blood will run.

She knew that escape from Germany was crucial. Indeed, by the end of 1933, 65,000 Germans had emigrated. The majority were Jews. Among them were Ruth's older sister Claire and her family. They went to France. Leni, Fritz and their little daughter would go to Palestine in 1935.

In late 1933 and for most of 1934 the initial rush of laws against 'non-Aryans' died down as Hitler turned his attention, for the moment, to the German Army. People like my father felt justified in their beliefs. Some who had fled even came back, preferring to live in their own country. Ruth was always aware of the urgency, but she was newly married, setting up a home, planning a family, and Fred had only just qualified. So they stayed, and I was born in December 1934, Tommy in November 1937.

*　*　*

April 1938

It is breakfast time in our apartment, Sedanstrasse 17a. Ruth is feeding Tommy with one hand, leafing through the *Newe Leipziger Zeitung* with the other. She stiffens.

'Fred, look at this!' He is helping me slice the top off my egg, a tricky operation we always enjoy; how much yolk will spill out? How much mess might we make?

'What?'

Ruth pushes the paper across the table.

'It says here we have to declare any assets or valuables over 5,000 Reichsmarks to a depot or pawnshop, it's not clear, near us. There's a date somewhere near the end.'

I am engrossed in my runny egg, but I can hear her voice sounds wobbly.

'We haven't got any valuables. You prefer arty jewellery to the real thing.'

She starts to clear the breakfast things; he gets ready to go to the hospital. They wonder what would be deemed as valuables that they might have. The walls of the apartment are lined with books. Are they supposed to shlepp them to a pawnshop?

'Your stamps!' Ruth exclaims. Fred looks doubtful.

25

'I don't know how valuable they are.'

'Exactly! You've been collecting since you were a boy. If we keep them we could be in trouble. I don't want to break any law. The cleaner, anyone could find them and tell the SS. Let me take the book to the shop, they might value it for us. I'll drop the children off. They can stay with Oma.'

This is the story my mother told us many times. Over the years different versions have emerged in the retelling from one generation to another, but this is what Tommy and I remember our mother telling us.

After making some inquiries Ruth found the shop. It was indeed a pawnshop situated in a side street, the window discreetly opaque. Outside the door two young apple-cheeked SS men were lounging, smoking and laughing at a shared joke. They made way for Ruth to pass through the door. Inside, behind the long counter, was an elderly, slightly stooping man, his back turned, examining the hive of crammed shelving behind. He turned sharply as the doorbell quivered. Ruth pushed the copy of the newspaper onto the counter, followed by the book of stamps.

'Uh! Huh!' he muttered, not looking at her. This was clearly not the first 'valuable asset' he'd taken in. He opened the stamp book and began to examine the contents with care, peering through his glasses and at times using a heavy magnifying glass. Ruth stood silent, worrying how long this would take. She had to pick us up and be home before the curfew at 2 p.m. when all Jews had to be indoors. Suddenly he looked her full in the face and smiled. Caught off guard she smiled back. My mother had an enchanting smile.

'This is a splendid collection. How long have you been...?'

'Oh! No, this isn't mine. It's my husband's. He's been collecting since he was a boy.'

'Well congratulate him for me. I'm something of an enthusiast

26

myself and I can appreciate another one.' His blue eyes were thoughtful as he gazed at her.

'I'm very sorry, Frau ...?'

'Bergmann.'

'Yes, Frau Bergmann, I am not happy at all. I have no choice.' His voice had sunk to almost a whisper. 'But I have to keep this book. I hope in better times it will be returned to you.'

Ruth, always so careful not to betray emotion in public, was moved by this man's kindness.

'I have two small children. This is only a stamp book.'

'I have to make an official note.' He turned to look for the documentation then quickly turned back, leaned over the counter and whispered rapidly.

'I have a proposition for you. We have to be very careful, my sons are standing outside the door. I have one stamp of great value. It will keep you and your family for all of your life. I like you and am sorry for what is happening to your people. Come back tomorrow, at this time. I will give it to you then.' He leaned back, found a pen, filled in the receipt, tore off the bottom copy for my mother.

'*Gutentag!*' Dismissing her, he turned back to his shelves.

What turmoil must her thoughts and emotions have been in? And what agonising must they have gone through that night? One tiny stamp would be easy to smuggle out.

'What if it's a trick to get me back there? His sons are both SS men. But he was kind. He seemed genuine. We'll need every penny to begin again. If we're caught ...! Think of the children.'

In the end Ruth remained true to her lifelong principle. 'I will not do anything illegal.'

She did not go back to the pawnbroker's shop. I hope he gave the stamp to someone else and gave them a new future.

By September 1938 all new purchases by Jews were taxed one hundred percent and all Jewish bank accounts had been closed. Furthermore, they were forbidden to buy jewels, ornaments and works of art. Prudently, my parents had spent all their savings before this happened. Considering his relative youth (he was only 31 in 1938), Fred was earning a high salary as a surgeon. Knowing that they would have to leave Germany, they had carefully planned and insured for our future. They bought clothes and shoes for Tommy and me up to the age of ten. Whether anything would have fitted or been to our taste we were never to find out. Fred bought the equipment for a small surgical unit, including 20 beds, an operating theatre with all the necessary instruments. Everything was packed into lifts (very large crates) and sent to Rotterdam ready to be shipped out to British Honduras. The plan was to set up a medical centre with Uncle Wilhelm (a dentist), and Aunt Erica who were also planning to go there. When the Germans invaded Holland in 1940 they confiscated everything. So maybe the stamp would have come in handy after all.

*   *   *

It was market day. Ruth pushed the pram patiently through the bustling crowd. Stalls piled high with seasonal fruit and vegetables and sausages, all different shapes and sizes, hanging thickly from butchers' hooks lined the street, and the air was pungent with aromas from the fish stall. Vendors shouted out their bargains, children squabbled, customers argued the price, but Ruth kept her eyes down, aware of the slowness of her little girl trying to keep up, clutching the pram handle with one small red mittened hand, the other thrust into her coat pocket. The baby (he'd just had his first birthday) peacefully asleep, golden curls tumbling round his rosy face. All three wore the obligatory scrap of yellow, shaped like a star, on their coats, Tommy's almost hidden by his blanket. She avoided eye contact: for fear of rejection from people she knew; for fear of abuse. The children had been spat at in the past.

'Can I have sweets, Mummy?'

'Yes, yes, later.'

She bought the provisions they needed quickly, no bargaining, no polite courtesies, as unobtrusively as possible, anxious to get home, safely within her four walls.

'You're going too fast. I'm tired. I want sweets.'

'We'll stop at the sweet shop. I promise, we won't be long. Don't make so much noise, please.'

Ruth made her final purchase at the butcher's stall. She had been buying meat here for several years. The transaction completed, she smiled briefly, 'Thank you.' Still holding the paper bag he leant forward.

'Frau Bergmann?' His voice low, urgent, the neutral smile fixed on his ruddy face.

'Yes?'

He fumbled with the bag, securing the fastening, eyes cast down.

'They're coming for Jewish doctors today.'

'Thank you.' She took the bag, her eyes met his and in that second she tried to convey her unspeakable gratitude. Friends like this were few.

'Come on, darling. Let's see if we can walk home very quickly, give Daddy a surprise.'

'But I want sweets!'

'Yes I know, but not today, not today.'

I remained silent, my legs pumping hard to keep up. I sensed there was more at stake here, I could feel my mother's fear as she pushed the pram as fast as she dared without running, without attracting attention. Opening the heavy front door, she frantically pulled the pram up the steep, narrow flight of steps to the entrance to our apartment, leaving pram and baby on the narrow landing.

'Fred, Fred, are you there?'

He came out of the bedroom sleepy eyed, yawning, he'd been operating most of the night.

'What is it? Calm down! Hello, darling, had a good walk?' He rumpled my hair and helped me peel off my mittens.

'You've got to get out, now, they're rounding up all Jewish doctors. Take a bag, anything. Go to the hospital … you can hide in the cellar if necessary. Don't stare and stand there … Don't you hear me? Go! Now!'

'They can't arrest me. I'm the only surgeon left in the Jewish hospital.'

'Fred, please listen. They can and they will. For my sake and the children be safe and go now.' Suddenly she ran to the stairs.

'The Steins. I must warn David.' She took the stairs two at a time to the second floor, ringing the bell, banging on the door. Anna Stein opened the door, bewilderment and fear etched on her face.

'Anna, they're coming for the Jewish doctors … warn David.' And she was already halfway down the stairs.

Fred was squatting on the floor, with me between his knees, a small bag ready by his side.

'Mummy will bring you to the hospital so I'll see you soon, maybe even later today.' He kissed me and got to his feet. 'Take care, Ruth.' She was by the window peering out through the net curtains. The trees lining the street were golden, beginning to shed their leaves. No sign of life except the familiar black saloon cruising up the street.

'They're here! The fire escape, go round the back!'

She grabbed my hand, dragged me out of the apartment, pushing the now wailing Tommy to the top of the narrow dark stairs just as the Gestapo burst open the front door. They waited politely, holding the door, as a small, rather stocky young woman very inexpertly bumped her pram step by clumsy step downwards, dragging a reluctant little girl and blocking their way entirely. As she finally reached the bottom step she gave them an apologetic smile and walked away.

* * *

Whilst our family was celebrating my brother Tommy's first birthday on 7 November 1938, elsewhere in Europe a 17-year-old German–Polish Jewish youth, Herschel Grynszpan, walked into the German embassy in Paris and shot the Third Secretary, Ernst vom Rath. Three days before, Herschel, at the time living with his uncle in Paris, had received the news that his parents, along with other Polish Jews had been deported to the small Polish border town of Zbaszyn, a no man's land, where they were left, stateless, homeless, many without food or shelter. Herschel Grynszpan's revenge for the fate of his family in Germany gave the Nazis the spark they had been looking for to unleash the pent-up hatred against the Jews long present in the community. The enforced segregation of a whole people and a vicious wave of propaganda paved the way for what became known as *Kristallnacht* (The Night of Broken Glass), a euphemism for what actually happened.

The pressure had been building up throughout 1938:

12 March

Hitler marches into Austria, unopposed, and announces the

'*Anschluss*', the merging of the two countries into one. The population of Austria is thus incorporated into the Third Reich, including nearly 200,000 Jews. Having forced almost that number out of Germany Hitler now has the same population to deal with as when he came to power in 1933. Drastic action is needed.

26 April

It is announced that all Jewish valuables and holdings over 5,000 Reichsmarks are to be registered. Six weeks later an inventory of all Jewish businesses is drawn up. This gives the Nazis a complete picture of Jewish assets.

28 May

In Frankfurt-am-Main, one of the oldest Jewish quarters, Jews are rounded up and subjected to a day of abuse, intimidation and degradation, much the same as had taken place in Vienna a month before. They are made to eat grass, climb trees, twitter like birds, scrub pavements, then forced to run in circles until they collapse. 'Pleasure hours' as the Nazis describe the day.

9 June

The main synagogue in Munich is burned down.

10 June

Dr Joseph Goebbels, Propaganda Minister, makes a secret speech to city police. 'In the coming half year, the Jews must be forced to leave Berlin. The police are to work hand-in-hand with the party in this.'

Throughout Germany 2,000 Jews are arrested and charged with 'race pollution'. Those arrested are taken to Dachau or to the recently opened concentration camp at Buchenwald near Weimar, where they are made to break and haul stones for 14 to 16 hours a day in what came to be known as 'the quarries of death'. During the summer and autumn the inmates of Buchenwald and Sachsenhausen, the camp near Berlin, are put to work enlarging the camps to receive thousands more prisoners. At Dachau, near Munich, prisoners are made to sew the Star of David on thousands of striped uniforms. The brutality in the camps, behind closed doors, is reported in the *London News Chronicle* describing the reception of 62 Jews, including two rabbis, taken to Sachsenhausen. At the gate, they were handed over by their police escort to SS camp guards, who forced them to run the gauntlet of spades, whips and clubs. An eyewitness described how the police, 'unable to bear their cries, turned their backs'. As the Jews were beaten, they fell. As they fell, they were beaten more. This orgy of violence lasted half an hour. When it was over, 12 of the 62 were dead, their skulls smashed. The others were all unconscious. The eyes of some had been knocked out, their faces flattened and shapeless. My parents, along with many other Jews, knew of these happenings and were becoming increasingly afraid as they waited for the next blow. Captain Frank Foley, the British chief passport control officer, of whom I shall write more later, urgently reported to London that it was 'no exaggeration to say that Jews had been hunted like rats in their homes, and for fear of arrest, many of them sleep at a different address overnight'.

10 August
The major synagogue in Nuremburg is torched.

17 August
All Jews have to take the name of Sara or Israel before their existing first names. I still have the four identity cards in which Ruth and I are 'Sara'; Fred and Tommy are 'Israel'.

27 September
Jewish lawyers are forbidden to practise in Germany.

7 October
All passports belonging to Jews (which already had a large 'J' in red stamped inside) are to be withdrawn and invalidated. They are to be replaced by special identity cards.

14 October
Hermann Wilhelm Göring, founder of the Gestapo and SA Commander, at a meeting with his colleagues, signals the need for more drastic action. 'The Reich must eradicate doubtful elements from the population – namely the last remaining Jews.'

*   *   *

During this time many nations were starting to close their doors, alarmed at the flood of refugees. Where could half a million Jews, my family amongst them, go? Certainly the Third Reich did not want us! The Nazis needed to take action quickly; they needed the right opportunity, the right time and the right stimulus to unleash the forces for one enormous, shattering blow. With perfect timing that opportunity was inadvertently handed to them by a 17-year-old youth in Paris, Herschel Grynszpan.

The murderous response to his action was carefully orchestrated. 'Spontaneous' demonstrations were to be organised, but the party was not to be seen as responsible. 'The SA should be allowed to have a fling,' Hitler was overheard to say. His strong-arm squads, the brown-shirted stormtroopers of the SA, the Sturmabteilung, could go into action without any constraints. The elite SS and Gestapo together with the regular police were to stand by and prevent looting (to ensure that Jewish possessions were safeguarded for the party) and protect buildings as soon as the owners had been evicted. They were to arrest 20,000 to 30,000 Jews, 'well-to-do Jews to be selected'.

The police had instructions to protect non-Jewish property, but synagogues could be burned as long as there was no danger of the fire spreading to the surrounding district.

On the night of 10 November every Jewish synagogue and most business premises and Jewish homes were wrecked or commandeered, 30,000 Jews were arrested and at least 100 killed.

In Leipzig events reflected the national scene. Possessions were thrown from upper windows, sometimes followed by their owners. People were hunted and thrown out of their homes, beaten and humiliated. Apartments and synagogues were torched. Businesses were ransacked or burned and the owners themselves arrested for this crime and sent to concentration camps. The rest of the world wrung their hands and did nothing.

Fred was already in the relative safety of the hospital and Ruth hurriedly packed the clothes we needed and took Tommy and me to join him.

We never returned to our apartment and very soon after leaving we saw, as we passed by, that another family had moved in. This, however, did not give my parents any concern. They had enough to worry about. The Gestapo, for reasons best known to them, did not close the hospital, but decided to make life as difficult as possible for my father to continue to operate. All other surgeons had been arrested. Fred was put under house arrest and only Ruth, with two small children to look after, had any freedom of manoeuvre. She wrote in her baby book for me, at a time that was so fearful and dangerous. Her tone is guarded yet she manages to be as positive as possible in unimaginable circumstances.

February 1939
'*My little daughter! Your fourth birthday passed rather quietly. So much has happened since I last wrote something and I will try to recollect events of the past months for this account.*

At the beginning of November we had to leave our flat and we are since living in Pappi's office in the Israel Hospital. It is quite big but of course too cramped for four people. On top of that you little thing are not one of the quietest and you are not very tidy. But you like it here very much. The nurses spoil you and you are never bored, so much is happening, which interests you.

You are getting on very well with Tommilein, and it is a great pleasure to watch the two of you. You are monitoring his progress with great delight and are very fond of him.

Unfortunately staying in the hospital is not good for you children. You can't roam around, can leave the room only when going for a walk, and the atmosphere is a constant source of danger for you.

Because I have to assist Pappi who has in the meantime become head of the surgical department I did not have time to go out with you. A very nice 14-year-old girl, Auntie Ilse, takes you for walks in the afternoon, and that has agreed with you very well so far.'

I remember Ilse a little from that time. She had very dark, almost black eyes like sparkly beads, and black tightly curled hair, and she laughed a lot. An energetic teenager, she must have welcomed the opportunity to look after us, take us to the park and generally babysit when both our parents were occupied. It rescued her from the tense atmosphere in her own home with elderly parents. Soon she would be sent to England with the Kindertransport. She had already passed her school matriculation, which would later make it possible for her to train as a nurse at Guy's Hospital in London. We remained in contact until her death in 2003. A courageous woman, she contracted polio in 1947 shortly after her marriage to a doctor at Guy's, a good, kind-hearted man and one of the ugliest I have ever seen. Sadly, she was unable to walk again. This did not deter her from having three children and eventually many grandchildren. Her brother, Peter, one year younger, was kept behind as his parents felt it was important for him also to have the matriculation before making a new start in England. Ilse never saw Peter or her parents again. There were so many stories of misjudged priorities, misplaced trust, misguided loyalty as the noose tightened slowly, slowly, until it was too late.

I have one distinct memory of my own. This was my daily interview with the resident Gestapo. There he would sit, jack boots on the table.

'Come in, little girl. Sit down. Tell me, what have you been doing today?'

Silence. I squeeze my lips tight shut.

'How about a little sweetie? Come on now, don't be shy.'

Shake of head.

'And how are your mummy and daddy? What have *they* been doing today?'

Silence.

And so on and so on. I had been well coached by my parents not to say anything. However, my four-year-old confidence remained undaunted. I believed that if Herr Hitler threatened me I would just dance for him, sing a little song and he would be so enchanted that he would let me and my family go free.

*   *   *

It is 11 November. The phone rings. Ruth answers. It is my paternal grandmother.

'Oma, what's wrong? Calm down. I can't understand you. Speak slowly. What? Where? No, just stay where you are. Don't go out … it's too dangerous. I'll talk to Fred. We'll do something. Try not to worry.'

'What is it?' asks Fred.

'They've arrested your father. They've taken him to the Festhalle. Oma says there are rumours that all the men will be taken by train to Buchenwald. They can't do that! He's over sixty. He's got a bad heart. My God, they can't do this!'

Ruth snatches her bag and coat. 'I'm going to the Festhalle. I'll get him back.'

And she did. Pushing her way through the dense crowd of anxious people waiting to hear news of husbands, fathers, sons, brothers, she battled her way right to the gates, shouting to the guards that she wished to see the man in charge immediately and waving her calling card at them. They must have been taken aback by such audacity but also had some admiration for her courage. They took her card and left her clinging on to the gates. A little while later an officer came out, her card in his hand and demanded to see her. What did she mean by this?

'You have arrested my father-in-law David Bergmann. He is over sixty, in poor health and you have no right to do this.'

'Go home, I'll see what can be done.'

Two days later he was released and back home.

38

On 16 November, due to severe overcrowding, Jews over 60, sick or physically handicapped, were ordered to be released from Buchenwald.

Another release, but of a very different nature, happened to a friend of Ruth's whose husband had also been arrested on *Kristallnacht*. The long awaited call came. 'Your husband is coming home ... expect him tomorrow.' What relief, what joy and anticipation! Then came the knock at the door. The official handed her her husband's ashes in a casket. The shock drove her to madness. Ruth was with her at the time. It was one of the stories I didn't want to hear in later years, but knew in my heart that it had to be told and retold.

A practical problem now arose. Fred could carry on operating, but his theatre sister had fled and her replacement had become ill. It was imperative for his own safety, for his patients and others that the procedures of the hospital, even though running down, be kept running as smoothly as possible. Ruth, with her experience as technician and assistant to doctors, plus her observations of operations when Fred was training, a quick learner, and a good actress, became the new theatre sister. Operations were carried out with the Gestapo observing. They never questioned her credibility.

The daily ward round took on a macabre aspect; the white-coated doctor accompanied by a nurse in her crisp white uniform and, following behind, the dark figure of another more ominous uniform.

The little procession comes to a halt in front of a female patient's bed.

'Please remove the dressings on this woman.'

'This patient is a French national. She is a dancer working here. You have no right to interfere with her treatment.'

'I wish to see if her operation is genuine. Remove the bandages now!'

'I'm sorry but I can't do that. She has had a mastectomy, she has cancer. She has gone through enough already. I have no intention of making matters worse for her.'

'This will go very badly for you, doctor.' The so far silent patient motioned Fred nearer to her.

'Please, doctor, take the dressing off. I don't want any trouble for you. Do what he wants.'

In this way my father's work was fraught with danger. He did hide people, sometimes by putting limbs in plaster. Ruth's parents were amongst these bogus patients. The French ballet dancer was a genuine case. Others, released from camps like Buchenwald, with heads shaved, filthy, starved and in shock were hidden in the cellar. They were the lucky ones who had some evidence such as visas, letters of invitation, so that they could leave Germany. Ruth would make scrambled eggs and they would wait until she was gone before they fell on the food. My Uncle Wilhelm, in Frankfurt, was in Buchenwald for four weeks while my Aunt Erica, even though she had the visas from the British Consulate for British Honduras, had to apply for their passports from the main police department and then file for Wilhelm's release from the Nazis. She describes him on his release in the account she wrote of their escape:

His head was shaved, his clothes so dirty and smelly we had to throw them out, and he was pale and hollow-eyed. The first week he mostly sat around staring, like he was in shock. He was more or less still in shock for the next two weeks. He would not tell me much about what he went through, partly because the Nazis threatened to get them if they talked about what happened.

It now became imperative for us to leave Germany. Ruth had been put in touch with the Quakers in England. They were actively helping people to leave. It had been decided that we would join my aunt, uncle and (paternal) grandparents who had already left for British Honduras. Ruth bought the tickets for one four-berth cabin on the *Simon Bolivar*, leaving from England in November 1939. The Quakers assured us that providing that we had temporary visas, they would guarantee our brief stay in England. Another practical problem now arose. Ruth needed to be free to get the visas. She could not be theatre sister, full-time mother and travel to the nearest British Consulate in Dresden. This is where Ilse's help proved invaluable. It was August, the school holidays, so she could look after Tommy and me, while Ruth now urgently sought for visas. As soon as she had the necessary invitation from Mr Howard of the Quakers she travelled to Dresden. The consulate refused to give her visas. Desperately, she took the next train from Leipzig to Berlin, turning down an offer from a friend to travel together on the next day – a life-saving decision as it turned out.

After hours of waiting in the palatial consulate on Wilhelm Strasse in Berlin, an official made the announcement to the hundreds of people waiting in the queue, 'Come back tomorrow. We are not giving any more visas today.'

There are moments when it becomes necessary to shape one's own destiny. This was my mother's moment. She did not leave. Sitting in a corner of the bustling hall, she waited. As the day's business began to come to a close a British official came over and spoke to her in his strongly accented German. 'Madam, I've noticed you sitting here for some time. You should go home.' And, seeing her tear-worn face, 'What is the matter?'

Ruth explained: she had two small children, a husband under

house arrest, they had to leave Germany. She had a letter from England. He listened. 'Give me the letter and your passports.' He disappeared into the nether regions of the building. Ruth found it hard to breathe. Could she trust this stranger? He had their passports and her life-saving letter from the Quakers. Ten minutes later he reappeared.

'I have your visa here.'

'And for my husband?'

'Yes.'

'And for my children?'

'Yes.'

She burst into tears. 'Thank you. Thank you.'

As she hurried down the marble steps she saw with horror the endless black snake of people winding down the road from the Consulate and the large notice attached to the gates 'British Nationals Only' and she knew that now only British passport holders would be allowed through those gates.

* * *

It was this scene at the consulate that my father so vividly remembered in his mid-eighties and which I have on tape. Throughout this story I am grasping at memories like wispy clouds drifting by, sometimes imagining dialogue from the bare facts my mother told me. But now and again I have solid blocks to build with. The last dialogue at the consulate, though not recounted by my mother is word for word from my father's lips. Later when a friend lent me the book *Foley* in 2005, further confirmation of so much that Ruth and Fred had told me of that terrible time was almost unbearable to read. I can hear my mother's voice, echoing in my head, 'This is how it was ... this is how it was.'

Michael Smith's book *Foley* on the life of Frank Foley tells the story of an unsung hero. Foley worked as a passport control officer in Berlin from 1920. His official remit was to filter 'undesirables' such as communists and agitators from entering the United Kingdom and the Commonwealth. However, this was a cover for his real role as MI6 Head of Station in the German capital. His witness of the increasing anti-Semitism and the rise of Nazism during the 1920s and the 1930s filled him with dismay and led to his saving thousands of Jews. He hid people in his home, visited concentration camps to get Jews out, helped to provide forged passports and ignored the rules to limit visas.

James Holborn, *The Times* correspondent describes the scene in Wilhelm Strasse after *Kristallnacht*:

> *Desperate Jews continue to flock to the British passport control offices in Berlin and elsewhere in Germany in the hope of gaining admission to Great Britain, Palestine or one of the Crown Colonies. A visit to the passport control office here this morning showed that families were often represented only by their women-folk, many of them in tears, while the men of the family waited in a concentration camp until some evidence of emigration could be shown to the Secret Police.*
>
> *While harassed officials dealt firmly but as kindly as possible with such fortunate applicants as had come early enough to reach the inner offices – about 85 persons were seen this morning – a far larger crowd waited on stairs outside or in the courtyard beneath in the hope of admittance.*

In the book Foley's wife, Kay, is quoted:

Jews trying to find a way out of Germany queued in their hundreds outside the British consulate, clinging to the hope that they would get a passport or a visa. Day after day we saw them standing along the corridors, down the steps and across the large courtyard, waiting their turn to fill in the forms that might lead to freedom.

In the end that queue grew to be a mile long. Some were hysterical. Many wept. All were desperate. With them came a flood of cables and letters from other parts of the country, all pleading for visas and begging for help. For them Frank's yes or no meant the difference between a new life and the concentration camps. But there were many difficulties. How could so many people be interviewed before their turn came for the dreaded knock at the door?

These were eyewitness accounts in 1938. When Ruth came to the consulate in the summer of 1939 the situation was increasingly hopeless.

Hubert Pollack, one of Frank Foley's secret agents, wrote:

Tens of thousands of Jews and non-Jews can thank Capt. Foley and his staff for their salvation. But unfortunately only a few of them are aware of this.

Was my mother one of these? The compassion of the official who took pity on her, the speed with which he produced the visas makes it possible that we owe our lives to this brave man and his helpers. It remains an unanswered question.

* * *

Do I believe in miracles? I ask myself the question as a non-believer, not even an agnostic. I was raised in a non-religious home. My parents, particularly my father, poured scorn on all organised religions. They followed their own unwritten creed of kindness and tolerance. And yet … and yet, looking back at my family's escape from Germany, two days before the outbreak of war, makes me wonder. Are there miracles? Is there a divinity, call it fate or destiny, taking care of us? And why only some of us?

Miracle one: In 1938 the industrialist Krupp was commissioned to build a large hospital in Afghanistan. They were recruiting doctors to go out there at the time when my parents were investigating any avenue of escape from the increasingly dangerous situation they were in. Fred applied for a job in Afghanistan. He had to send in our passports with the application form. Thus it was that when the edict that all Jews must hand in their passports was decreed ours were out of the country, and he could not hand them over to the authorities. Notification of the return of the passports came on New Year's Eve. Ruth raced to the local post office. It was vital that our passports did not fall into Nazi hands.

'Sorry, we're closing now – no more business till the New Year.' She begged, pleaded, flirted, used all the charm and acting skills that had disarmed the guards at the Festhalle and rescued her father-in-law, and which thus far had saved her husband from arrest.

'I've left my little children specially to get here, it's quite a journey. Come on, it's New Year's Eve, be a good chap, it won't take a minute and you'll end the year well, doing a real kindness, please, please.'

And once again she succeeded. If the passports had remained in official keeping they would have been confiscated.

Miracle two: The scene is the reception area of the hospital. Fred, always rushing and energetic, breezes through, his stethoscope hanging out of the pocket of his white doctor's coat. 'Just going out for a packet of cigarettes.' He smiles at the Gestapo guards engrossed in a game of cards. They nod vaguely and carry on. They have never seen my father smoke. He has never smoked. He was then and remained all his life a vehement opponent of smoking. But 'the packet of cigarettes' got him out, straight to the railway station where we were waiting for him and onto the train for Holland, freedom and safety.

Miracle three: The train arrives at the Dutch border, then stops. Border controls perhaps, a normal procedure? Suddenly there are German officials on the platform, some in uniform. 'Everyone out!' they shout. 'Get off the train, hurry, all out!' comes the command over and over again. People stumble out of the carriages, some bemused, others with taut, strained faces attempting to assume an indifference that is far from felt. Wisps of smoke drift over, the engine hisses and the acrid smell mixes with the smell of fear. Murmurs and mumbling like Chinese whispers snake up and down the platform as the crowd thickens, as the train empties. 'Who are they looking for?' 'Is it Jews?' 'Is it gypsies, social democrats, communists?'

'Border control, have your passports ready,' comes the order. Relief escapes like a long sigh along the platform as the passengers give in their passports and form an orderly queue to retrieve them. A more relaxed atmosphere ensues. People chat, even laughter is heard. My father's turn comes, my mother, holding Tommy on one arm and me by the hand (I can feel her shaking) stands behind him.

'Bergmann?' The Dutch official, his peaked cap pushed down

over his forehead, thumbs through the passports in front of him. 'Sorry ... stand aside ...'

'But ...' my father splutters.

'Sorry ... can't find it ... stand back ... this won't take long.' The line shortens, people are getting back on the train. Still the official can't find our passports. We can see Holland, safety, life over the border.

'The train is going to leave,' my father exclaims, white, tight-lipped. 'Please find our passports, now.'

The whistle blows; the train begins to move. We stand on the platform, alone, as it pulls out of the station. The official shakes his head in disbelief, looking at the empty counter in front of him.

'I can't think what I did with it.' He taps his breast pocket hopefully, then puts his hand in his trouser pocket and triumphantly pulls out two passports. 'Must have slipped them in at the beginning in the rush, sorry.'

'But what are we to do? We need to get to Holland. We can't go back!'

Even as I write, 64 years later, I am shaking.

'Oh! Don't worry, you can wait for the next mainline train or ...' He pauses, now smiling at us benignly. 'There's a little local Dutch commuter train, should be here in half an hour.'

It came and we crossed the border to safety. The next mainline train to leave Germany for Holland was searched at this border. All Jews were taken off.

So you can see how the 'if' factor has haunted my life. If my mother hadn't been persistent and strong, if the Gestapo had noticed that my father was a non-smoker, if Krupp had not built a hospital in Afghanistan and if there hadn't been a little local train ...

47

4

England

I have a feeling of lightness as I start this chapter. I certainly did not feel it on the day we left. We were now refugees. Where would we go? What would happen to us?

Now, decades later, I sit in my cosy little study, my cats companionably curled up nearby and I feel an enormous relief. We are out of Germany! We've made it!

We left Holland on the ferry to Harwich on 26 August 1939. My four-year-old senses absorbed the anxiety my parents felt: Ruth's anxiety at leaving Oma and Opa behind in Holland to face the ever increasing possibility of invasion; the uncertain future facing us.

On 1 October, a few weeks after our arrival in England, Ruth wrote:

A very hard time lies behind us. As Jews we were forced to leave Germany. Unfortunately our attempts to emigrate were often unsuccessful. At the last moment we managed to get a visa for England. Eight days after our speedy and hurried departure from Germany the war between England, France on one side – Germany on the other broke out. You, Bobbilein and Tommilein don't know, thank G. anything of all the worries, all the disasters which are behind us, and what war means. Gott sei Dank nicht!

The journey, which was an escape – from Germany through Holland (where we visited the grandparents Frankenberg in Dieren for a day) to England was extremely stressful for you. But you were always sweet and good.

We had just that one day with my grandparents. They had only recently arrived in Holland. Ruth, fearful for their safety in Markgrafenstrasse after 11 November, had managed to get them admitted to the hospital. For three weeks she worked tirelessly to get the required documents for them to travel to the relative safety of Holland, where they had some distant family who would take them in. They went, as Fred put it, 'from bed to train', smuggled out of the hospital under the eyes of the resident Gestapo.

I have only two photographs of my grandparents, one a happy family group taken before I was born, with my grandfather waving his cigar and looking delighted with his other grandchildren around him. The other is of the two of them with me, aged three, my grandfather standing, tall and elegant, my grandmother sitting, smiling with her arms around me. I am clutching my teddy bear. It was the last time we saw Oma and Opa, a poignant parting in a country preparing for war with gun emplacements on street corners, and everywhere stacks of sandbags.

We had only been allowed 10 marks per adult when we left so friends of my grandparents had collected a little cash to send us on our way.

The memory of my first experience of being on a boat at sea is of an all-pervading sadness, like a sea mist enveloping us all.

From the port we took the train to Manchester, arriving late at night to a city already in black out. It was very dark, no welcoming lights anywhere. Too late to meet with our Quaker saviour, Mr Howard.

Fred investigated the few hotels around the station and quickly realised that we couldn't afford any of them, so we settled down in the station waiting-room to spend the night. Fred was deeply asleep when he felt a hand on his shoulder. Rudely awakened, he faced a man in uniform and an instant fear.

'Sorry, sir, but you can't sleep here, you know. This is the ladies waiting-room. Gents have to sleep on the platform.'

Relief flooded through my father. If this was the only stricture he faced in this new country he was a happy man.

'Pretty children,' the station master added with a nod to our sleeping forms as he left. My father was deeply touched, he was used to his children being spat at. He spent the rest of the night sleeping peacefully on a bench on the platform.

An insight into the madness of those dark days was the contents of the one small suitcase we brought with us. A change of clothing for Tom and me and an ivory satin ball gown for Ruth and tails for Fred. I never saw Ruth in the dress, but I remember seeing a photograph of her wearing it in Leipzig looking very glamorous with the butterfly shoulders and low décolletage. She probably sold it for much needed cash soon after we arrived. The story goes that my Aunt Erica, in British Honduras, where we were due to go, had told them that it was most important to have formal dress if and when invited to the governor's dinners. Even in the haste and drama of leaving was this seen as a priority? We had no warm coats, nothing at all practical for the winter ahead. It was always referred to later with a mixture of hilarity and disbelief.

Next morning Mr Howard met us at the station. We sat together in the buffet over mugs of tea and, as I see it now, our future, whether we lived or died, was decided.

'I don't think you should go to British Honduras,' said Mr Howard. 'The climate is severe, not good for little children. You'd do much better to stay here.'

My parents were taken aback. They had tickets for the ship. They had family already in British Honduras. They knew no one in England. Ruth remembered her father's love of English traditions, the breakfasts, English tea, Saville Row and her own love of the literature.

Mr Howard continued to persuade.

'You could make a good life here. Doctors will be needed, particularly surgeons. And think of your children, they might suffer in an inclement climate. In fact I really want you to think carefully and stay here. Meanwhile I'm putting you on a train to Marple, there's a hostel there for German refugees.'

I wasn't privy to the soul searching or the final decision but it was decided that for the time being we remain in England. Fred sent the tickets for the four-berth cabin on the *Simon Bolivar* to a family he knew of in Holland, mother, father and two children, desperate to leave. They must have been overjoyed to receive those tickets.

The *Simon Bolivar* was the first civilian ship to be torpedoed by the Germans in the war. Only the mother of the family of four survived.

The effect of all that happened in those few months from November 1938 to September 1939 has left me with an enduring gratitude and a zest for living. Our mother engendered in us the philosophy of 'live for the day'. In spite of all the sorrow and anxiety, she was always full of fun and enthusiasm. She baked a lot and when we greedily ate everything she would say, 'What we have today we don't have tomorrow, so eat and enjoy.'

* * *

The following is taken from Ruth's book to me, translated from the German, written in the hostel in Marple in October 1939:

Norwood, Arkwright Road
Wonderful people, the Quakers, helped us to leave the
country in which we had hell. They have given us a new home
here in a hostel ... and we are eternally grateful. We can feed
you two chaps well, healthily and sufficiently, which means
very, very much for us as parents. Before the war, Germany
had already food shortages for some time, so that would
have been impossible. After Kristallnacht German retailers
were forbidden to serve Jewish customers. Often kind
neighbours or other non-Jewish friends would shop for
them. You both look very well and are eating well. But we
worry about you being rather pale. In comparison with
Tommy who always has red cheeks you are much frailer in
appearance. Unfortunately you had a slight throat infection
which cleared with tablets Pappi prescribed.

For me, Marple consisted of just one road, with four houses. Each one holds special memories. I'm sure there was more to it, shops and a station for instance, but they didn't exist for me. The houses were immense, quite beautiful, except for the hostel where we had a room. It was a gloomy square building, with lots of windows and dark shrubbery all around, not a proper garden as the others had. Our room was square with a square window. The house was full of women and children; all the men were taken away to be interned first in Liverpool and then the Isle of Man as potential enemy aliens.

Our parents had explained to us that Fred, with all the other men, would have to go away for a while, so I was not unduly alarmed on the night the police came for my father. I knelt on the window-sill to see the man in the strange hat at the front door. My father had a little bag; he waved up to the window to say 'Goodbye'. Ruth came into the room, crying, and at that moment a mouse ran diagonally across the square wooden floor. She screamed and screamed. A mouse succeeded where the Gestapo had not. It demonstrates her new-found sense of security that she allowed herself this moment of panic. I had never seen a mouse before and have had an illogical terror of them ever since.

Every day the women would crowd around the wireless to listen to the news, interpreting as best they could what they heard in the new language. One day my mother rushed up to our room, threw herself on the bed and cried and cried and cried. I was afraid she'd never stop, the sobbing and shaking seemed to go on for days, and I didn't know what to do. How I wished my father was there! It was only later, when she was calmer, that she explained that the German Army had marched into Holland. She did not tell me then that the Dutch had capitulated in five days; that she knew that along with thousands of other Jews her parents would be rounded up and arrested. And she did not know until after the war ended in 1945 what had happened to them. My grandfather, mercifully, died in Holland of a heart attack and is buried in Arnhem on the German border. Oma was taken first to Theresienstadt in Czechoslovakia and then to Auschwitz where she was killed in the gas chambers.

Further down from our hostel was Mrs Brown's house. There was no Mr Brown; he must have gone to fight in the war. Mrs Brown was tall and slim. Her complexion was creamy, everything about her, her hair, her clothes, was fair.

I had only ever known our apartment in Leipzig with a communal yard, and then the one room in the Jewish hospital, so to me a whole house was a wonderment. Mrs Brown's was enormous and light with large airy rooms, and the garden was even more exciting: lawns spreading all around, flower beds overflowing with colour, different trees, some weeping, others reaching upwards and space, space in abundance.

We played with Mrs Brown's children – a boy and a girl – on the lawns and she gave me her little girl's clothes, pleated skirts with a big safety pin at the front edge and pullovers with blue and green and yellow patterns knitted in. One day they had a birthday party for her daughter. We were invited. I announced to the assembled guests, in my hesitant English, that I was the prettiest girl there. My mother was mortified and very angry with me when we got back. I was sent to bed in disgrace and the phrase 'I must knock the conceit out of you' was born.

The third important house was almost opposite Mrs Brown. This was Mrs Budenberg who became our benefactress and one of my godmothers. This house was also huge but darker and full of rich, heavy furniture. There were trees surrounding the front, and the back was endless, rolling down through woodland to a railway embankment. Where Mrs Brown had open sunny spaces, here there was mystery and a hint of danger. Mrs Budenberg was old and small and wrinkled and she always took afternoon tea with her sister, Mrs Wigglesworth, served at a little table with shiny silver and pretty cups and saucers. I had my own sturdier cup. Mrs Wigglesworth, who looked like her sister, kept her hat on for tea, which I thought was what lady visitors did in England.

These two kind and generous women offered to adopt Tommy and me in the event of a German invasion, an ever present threat in those months, late 1939, early 1940. They suggested that we were both baptised so we would have legal documentation that we were not Jews. Ruth and Fred would have to make their own way, though where they could escape to on a relatively small island is hard to imagine. I have no memory of any ceremony, but Tommy and I were baptised into the Church of England, and our parents must have felt some relief that we would be safe.

However, at the time I was much more interested in Mrs Budenberg's big, shiny black car and the man in uniform who drove it. This man and his vehicle had an important part to play at this time in our lives. They took my mother to the Manchester Infirmary when she got very sick with her gall bladder. It was the time of the blitz and we could hear the bombs falling on the city and see the reddened sky from Marple. The people at the hostel planned to have Tom and me put in an orphanage, they didn't want the bother of looking after us (none of these families were Jewish). As a child I was not aware that my mother was very unhappy in this hostel, facing animosity from the other refugees. This is evident in my father's letters from internment at this time. '*Do not be angry about the other people and keep fit and as well as possible.*' And in another letter; '*Do not be worried at other people's views and stick to your own. We have quite different ideas and they cannot understand us. Therefore do not take any notice of all these "good advisers". They do not want to see you happier or more loved and that's that.*'

Fortunately, Mrs Budenberg, together with Mrs Brown, made sure we were properly looked after in the hostel until our mother came back.

When, in the spring of 1941, we moved to Macclesfield, the big car and kind driver continued to play an important part, arriving at our little rented house filled with the essentials we didn't have, cutlery, china, bedding.

When I was about seven and we were settled in Macclesfield, Mrs Budenberg invited me back to Marple to stay for a few days. She sent the big, black car with her chauffeur to fetch me. I was ready, clutching my small bag with pyjamas and toothbrush, my ears ringing with my mother's admonitions.

'Now be good, behave nicely, say thank you and please. They have been so good to us, you are a very lucky girl to have this little holiday, have a lovely time.'

With a mixture of pride, excitement and fear I got into the back of the car and we were off.

Mrs Budenberg had other guests staying with her, probably members of her family. They were grown up and didn't include me in their conversation. After supper, I was tucked up in a strange room, in an unfamiliar bed. Mrs Budenberg came to say goodnight with a large bottle of brown liquid in her hand. She poured out a big spoonful and came towards me.

'There we are, dear. You have this. It's good for you.'

'I don't want it.'

'Now come along. All good girls have this. Now don't make a fuss.'

'I don't want it.'

I remembered the stories I had heard and read about wicked godmothers who poisoned little girls and boys, and I struggled to avoid the horrible sticky brown fluid being forced down my throat.

'That's a good girl. Now you go to sleep. Goodnight, dear.'

The light was switched off, the door closed. I cried myself to sleep, wanting my mother, my home, even my brother and waiting for the poison to start working and to die a horrible death.

The following morning I found my way down to the dining-room. The other guests, there must have been three or four, were already there, laughing and joking around the long table.

'Good morning, Renée. Did you sleep well?'

I nod, 'Yes.'

They decide to have a little sport with me.

'You know the woods by the railway line?'

I nod, 'Yes.'

'Well, there are wolves there, and if little girls are naughty they come up in the night and eat them up!'

Well, that did it! The choice between another poisonous dose and being eaten by wolves was too much.

My mother was amazed to see the smart car pull up outside her door. I was brought back, red-eyed, the day after I had left.

However, this didn't spoil my earlier memories of Marple. I have left the best till last. A short walk from the hostel, in the opposite direction from Mrs Brown, was my first school. The headmistress was Mrs Hutton, a tall, broad woman, who sailed like a stately galleon through the school. She had a large bun at the back of her neck and wispy grey hair round her kind face, and her glasses twinkled with merriment as if her eyes and the world outside reflected each other. I loved her. I loved the school and every moment I was there. My reports commented on the improvement in my English and were generally good. But at the end of the term Mr Hutton, as kind and gentle as his wife, had to carry me back to the hostel, weeping copiously, after I had refused to leave the classroom. In one of Ruth's few surviving letters she refers back to this episode to Fred in the internment camp at Huyton, Liverpool, dated 28 September 1940.

Did I tell you that Renée awfully cried about the holidays? The teacher brought her home, feeding her with sweets, in his arms.

58

In August 1940 we (Ruth, Tommy and I) moved to Cheadle Hulme. There are two references to this in the minute book of the Refugee Committee of the Society of Friends (the Quakers' organisation) in the Manchester and District Area:

31 Jul. 1940 Min. 4 It was felt that Mrs Bergmann and family would be better accommodated at the Cheadle Hulme Hostel.

27 Aug. 1940 Min. 5 Mrs Bergmann and children have been happily transferred from Marple to Cheadle Hulme.

I have one vivid memory of this place. I did not go to school. But almost every night was spent in the hostel cellar. I had a small top bunk. It is the smell that has remained with me and is synonymous with the drone of planes and distant bangs. That musty, dank underground smell reminiscent of green fungi and clammy walls. Every time since then that I have been in a cellar that time leaps back and I can feel my mother's trembling hand dragging me down, down into this underworld, to be lifted into the bunk, wrapped in a blanket and told, 'Now, try to sleep.'

It is Ruth's account of that time that is most moving. It wasn't until 1945, at the end of the war, that she took up her pen again and this is what she wrote:

We ourselves have had difficult times here as well. (This was a reference to her sister and her family in France, with whom she had just made contact.) *Fred was interned for seven months like all foreigners and we three moved from Marple to a hostel in Cheadle Hulme. For almost five months we slept in the basement because of air raids and you were more often ill than well. It was really a very difficult time for me because I had gall bladder problems again, first time since your birth, because of the stress; and life in hostels was rather difficult, even unbearable, as the food was rationed, over priced and difficult to come by. The Quakers of course were always good and helpful, but it was most unpleasant to live, with small children, among refugees, who were poor, ill, unhappy and discontented. Everybody was on edge, everybody full of sorrows, and people lived together who would never have got together in normal circumstances.*

We visited our Pappi twice in the camp, and what a joy it was when he came back to us one evening in January. I am glad to say that you children never had the slightest fear because I always told you that the raids were exercises by English fighters, [I never believed her, sensing her fear, and I am happy that she felt her deception had worked] *therefore you took bombs and anti-aircraft noise rather calmly. For you the war happened in Germany, long, long before the outlook changed for the better, while Pappi in internment and I in the ice cold hostel cellar thought about what to do if the Germans attacked England. Would it be possible to escape ... without financial means? Would we see our Pappi again? Would Hitler win anyhow and our escape was in vain? One thing I knew, I would never have let you fall into the hands of the Nazis.*

We know now that everything turned out differently, and when you read this book you two will, I hope, be quite happy souls who can enjoy their lives in times of peace.

It no longer feels good for me to write in German, therefore I shall continue from now on in English.

5

Internment

My father was interned in two different camps. From May 1940 in Huyton, Liverpool and then from October 1940 until January 1941 at Sefton Camp, Douglas, on the Isle of Man. He was allowed to write two letters a week, on a prison issue, single narrow sheet, folded three ways with CENSORED stamped large on the back. No other paper was permitted. Thirty of his letters were carefully kept by my mother, only two of hers remain. The earliest, now almost illegible, are written in English. Later he reverts to German, perhaps for ease and greater intimacy. Their correspondence starts in July and I was puzzled by the preceding weeks of silence. The records of the Society of Friends' German Emergency Committee 1933–50 provide the explanation and cast some light on the stressful situation my parents and others were under at that time.

> *The suddenness in which these measures* [internment] *were carried out and the wholesale break-up of family life which resulted bore particularly hard on the refugees. For them the situation was unpleasantly reminiscent of what they had been through in Germany; having already proved at some cost their opposition to Hitler, or at least Hitler's opposition*

to them, it was a bitter experience to have their anti-Nazism thus called into question. At first no letters or newspapers were allowed into the camps and there was extreme delay in censoring outgoing post. Weeks passed, therefore, without refugees and other enemy aliens hearing from relatives or knowing their whereabouts.

The following is from the earliest letter that I have from Huyton, dated 9 July. It is barely legible.

My Dearest Kelchen [little lads] *I have not heard anything from you. Have you got my first letter and passport, etc.? I am on a special list for permanent emigration and for joint application for all those internees to be released to the ship. Therefore, try to get all our papers and the tickets that we can meet at the ship soon. Apply to War Office for visitors permit to have because of urgent talk with me about emigration.*

All of my father's letters affirm his concern for Ruth and us, and how much he misses us. He worries about her health, about the future. How devastated he must have been when he eventually heard the news of the fall of Holland in May and was not even able to comfort her.

In the camp at Huyton, Liverpool, my father was number 53159. He describes his circumstances and reassures her that he is well. He shared a space with four men who became firm friends (the number depleted when two of them left for a camp near London to wait for their visas to America). They got up at eight, breakfast was at eight-thirty, lunch at one and tea at six. They went to bed at ten. The rest of the day was spent reading, washing and cleaning, learning English and '*registering for this list and that application*'. And they played cards and chess. Fred reassures Ruth that he is comfortable. Initially he asks her not to make any hasty decision regarding British Honduras, Australia or anywhere else, just to get him out of the camp, but rather think only of our family and the future.

He suggests Ruth should not bring us to visit Huyton, as he fears we would be '*shocked by the barbed wire and the guards*'. He consistently asks her to save any money she has for emergencies (we received two and sixpence pocket money a week from the Quakers); not to spend money on him. Almost every letter begs her not to send any more parcels; he has enough of everything, enough to last till his release. But he does ask for a towel, dishcloths, apples and toilet paper. And at another time, Ryvita and '*perhaps a little jam?*'. And white thread for underwear repair.

Ruth, in her letter (28 September 1940) also reassures him that we are well, but her unhappiness at their separation is evident.

Today it is Sunday. I don't like it now, as I cannot hope for a letter from you. I hope you are well, liebstes [dearest]. *The children and I are very well. This night I dreamt suddenly you came home and I was so glad. But it wasn't so, and I was very sad, when I awoke . Unfortunately I got a refusal from the War Office, so I cannot visit you, Lumpchen* [their mutual term of endearment]. *When shall we come together again? Sometimes I think we cannot suffer more. We are always waiting for a happy time in our life and now we are separated it is too hard. I don't dare to think about my parents and Clare's family* [Ruth's sister Clare, her husband and two daughters were in France].

As his anxiety to rejoin his family grew, Fred's letters are increasingly dominated by instructions to Ruth to pursue every avenue for our immediate migration to obtain his release. Canada, Australia, Brazil – '*I think Brazil is for non-Catholics too*' – are mentioned. He asks her to inquire about a shipping company 'Elders and Fyfield' with banana steamers going via Guatemala. It is clear at this stage they had not decided to stay here. Why? Did the threat of imminent invasion make England potentially as dangerous as Germany had been? Was this the reason for his constant admonitions to her to contact anybody and everybody for help, affidavits and advice? It doesn't take a lot of imagination to understand his feeling of helplessness, unable to contact anyone himself and knowing the burden of responsibility he was putting on her.

Ruth was inundated with tasks to carry out for our emigration. Without the necessary documents, visas, permits from the place of destination, exit permits, Fred's internment could be a long one. There were instructions to apply to the War Office, the Home Office, The Society of Friends, for visitor permits and exit permits. She had to wire the family in British Honduras for affidavits; to seek advice from everyone regarding qualifications he needed for England, the USA, British Honduras, Australia. And then there were the requests to other wives for items their husbands needed; and thank yous to everyone for letters, parcels, support (he had no means to do so himself). She was charged with remembering his family's birthdays, names and dates listed; with buying a trunk, with his advice as to the contents for our departure: towels, woollen blankets, soap, knives, forks and spoons. There were requests for medical books so he could start to study in English (in September he learned that he could train as a specialist in tropical diseases, which would entitle him to work in the British colonies). And then suddenly in August 1940 he writes: '*I should like to stay here. The camps in central Australia seem to be extremely bad.*' In response to a letter from Ruth he again reiterates: '*I would also much prefer to live in England than in America or British Honduras.*'

In all his letters Fred's frustration and unhappiness at having to delegate his role as head of the family to burden Ruth is manifest. And often the decisions have to be hers. In response to the query whether it would be easier to get qualifications for British Honduras than Australia he writes, '*You will, however, know best what to do under the present circumstances and I leave it to you to decide.*'

Ruth had to function in a new language, with very limited resources for telephoning, stamps or travel. Wiring information is often mentioned, particularly to the family in British Honduras. I assume this was a cheap, fast way of communicating.

Yet in spite of all the responsibility put on her, in spite of constant illness with her gall bladder, Ruth still finds the time, energy and money to keep Fred supplied with clothes, home-made cakes and photos of us to cheer him up in a weekly parcel, plus her regular letters (every other day).

In September 1940 forced transportation of the interned men became another immediate danger, threatening our separate migration. As detailed in Lawrence Darton's *The Work of the Friends Committee for Refugees and Aliens 1933–50*, 4,000 men were transported to Canada, 2,000 to Australia, many without the knowledge of their closest relatives in this country. Fred would have known of the fate of the *Arandora Star*, bound for Canada with 2,000 Italian and German internees, including refugees on board, which had been torpedoed and sunk with the loss of most lives, when he wrote this letter:

I know almost for certain, unfortunately, that emigrants are released only to the ship directly and are not allowed to see even to important matters outside. Only force will be able to separate me from you and the children.

The postscript at the bottom of his precious piece of paper, written in English, reflects Fred's feelings:

Dear censor; if you have a wife and children far away from you in these dangerous days, you would – I am sure – not leave them without dropping a line to soothe their anxiety. Therefore don't delay this letter, please.
Thank you.
Dr. Bergmann.

My brother remembers our father telling him, many years later, how he hid in the camp when the officers came around compiling lists for deportation. This was 1940, England was fighting for its very existence, with the aerial Battle of Britain and the evacuation from Dunkirk, and the plight of refugees was, understandably, not high on the agenda.

To his great credit Winston Churchill had promised that in the event of an invasion, the interned Jewish refugees would immediately be released to fend for themselves, unlike the equivalent situation in France were they were handed over to the occupying forces. The fear of invasion prompted Ruth and Fred's acceptance of Mrs Budenberg's and Mrs Wigglesworth's generous offer to have Tom and me baptised into the Church of England, giving us the necessary documentation, and their promise that they would adopt us if the worst happened.

In September 1940, because of the heavy bombing on Liverpool, the internees were moved to the Sefton camp on the Isle of Man. They took over a large hotel and the physical circumstances greatly improved.

Much has been documented about the internment camp on the Isle of Man. Some of the internees have become famous and influential figures in politics, the arts and science. The combination of experience, knowledge and talent was rich. It was quickly realised by the authorities that the genuine refugees were far from enemies and they were treated accordingly, and, within the confines of the camp, were given considerable freedom. There were German spies and Nazis at the camp: men who elected to work in the kitchen and were found smuggling letters and information in the ashes of the stove. They were closely guarded and eventually deported.

On the tape I recorded, my father remembers, among other things, the concerts in which lasting partnerships were forged, later to become renowned ensembles with people like Ravitch and Landauer and the Amadeus Quartet. Every night there were lectures covering a wide variety of subjects. Fred lectured on anatomy and surgery. They were allowed to buy provisions and a café was established, coffee with Viennese pastries partaken of in the afternoons. And, of course, there was football, football, football. Fred sustained an injury at this time, which, sadly, ended his footballing days. He does not mention the incident in any of his letters, and he would explain to us children later that he didn't really mind, he'd reached the age when he would have stopped playing anyway.

I remember the chuckle in my father's voice when he told me how the guards would take them to visit the town. The order would be given, 'Left turn!' The trusted refugees would smartly 'right turn!' and be free to roam until the guards came back. They even went to the pictures! '*By the way, we went to the cinema yesterday, outside the barbed wire, like real human beings.*'

Fred had his own small room in the camp hospital where he was able to work for the medical services and to study. It was warm and there were clean sheets on the bed. In fact he said he could have been quite happy there. But of course, without us, he wasn't. He gave a weekly lecture on surgery in a rota with six other scientists. He writes that there is a small medical library available and very nice colleagues. His talent to make things was allowed to flourish. He designed and wove a scarf for Ruth's birthday in November: '*Mr. C.* [a fellow internee] *bought himself a small loom and I borrowed it for a while. I am really proud of my first attempt, especially of the pattern.*' In December he sent a small parcel home, I have forgotten the contents, but a hundred similar parcels were sent to children in Coventry, where the bombing was particularly ferocious, with items made by Fred and his fellow internees.

As the end of 1940 drew near the questions became more urgent. What happens when the temporary permit for British Honduras runs out? The banana boats to the West Indies will finish sailing at the end of December. Who will pay for the journey – The Society of Friends?

Fred asks: '*Would you approve of having our luggage sent to the USA if the organisation there would meet all the costs because this can only be paid over there? Please send your view in a nutshell.*'

When exit to the USA is terminated as the boats are all booked, Fred writes, '*Not to worry. Our case is different, we are going to South America, not the USA.*'

Reading through these letters I am filled with a growing despair at the constantly changing scenario: their hopes, like jelly fish, swept backwards and forwards on a relentless tide; the possibilities for emigration opening then closing; the mountain of bureaucracy that needs to be climbed. And ever present, the fear of invasion and the sheer misery of separation. And I admire Fred's strength and encouragement to Ruth. His letters, so full of concern, anxiety and love, always end with, '*Be brave; Keep smiling; Head high*'.

And he had much to be anxious about. On his birthday, 12 October, he was summoned to the commandant's office to receive an emergency phone call from Mr Howard. Ruth, now in Cheadle Hulme, had had a second gall bladder attack. Fred immediately put in a request for parole and leave under guard to be able to look after her and us. He stressed that he knew her medical history better than anyone, that he had been present at her operations in Leipzig. Permission was refused. He fretted about who would look after Tommy and me, so Ruth could recover. He wrote to her to rest, stay warm, not to save on heating. At other times he worried that we should have enough sandbags in the shelter; did we have the new gas mask filters, did we have good shoes, warm coats? Were we eating properly, was there enough fruit? Over and over again he urges Ruth to take care of herself, not to rush about too much (and yet he was depending on her to do just that!), eat well, keep warm, use the second bar on the electric fire. His love for her, his optimism and encouragement shine through these letters, and the oft repeated phrase '*Head high*' makes me want to weep.

*   *   *

We only had two visits in the seven odd months and so much anticipation must have gone into each one. In the second of Ruth's

69

two remaining letters, dated 5 September and written in English, she describes the restrictions on her own movements: '*I hope soon to get permission from the Chief Constable to enter protected area and then I shall send a telegram to you.*' She goes on to reassure him of our good health and describe our improved conditions in the new hostel in Cheadle Hulme:

I am very careful with the children. We have a lot of blankets on our mattress and the children are fully dressed in the cellar. I got a warm training dress [I think this was a siren suit] *from the Friends and over it I wear my raincoat. You will see how healthy and good our children are looking. Beside the very good food, they have their order like at home. They may go in the dining as well as the sitting room. Our big kitchen is also a nice place and very clean.*

And then she writes about the forthcoming, precious visit to the camp:

You will believe me that we three are not talking about other things than about our visit to you. When people tell us it will be exciting we say – we shall not see anything besides our good dear Pappilein. We shall be there punctually at 2 o'clock p.m. The permit says on the 10th between 2–5.30 p.m.

I shall bring the 2 excerpts of the pathological book with me. In the case [sic] *you want it I shall leave it, otherwise I shall take it back with me.*

All the best for you, liebster, bester. I embrace you (in 5 days in reality!!!) and give you a lot of kisses.
Yours ever, Ruth.

Fred was also filled with anticipation. Yet the letter he wrote two days after our visit was one of the rare moments when he let his own feelings come through:

My beloved little Rascal and my two Precious Ones! Yesterday I was rather sad to be without you once more, and unfortunately I am much more aware of the dreadful separation than before. I am afraid I didn't really enjoy your visit fully, talked too much and was not as nice to you as I had wanted to be. Don't be cross with me because of that, please; I was inwardly more moved than I could admit to myself. Hope you were not too exhausted when you got home. Was Bobbelchen [his nickname for me] *still very excited? I cannot forget Tommy's little squeaky voice for one minute, even less his sleepwalking after my departure. Many thanks, my brave little lad, for all your great love.*

Tommy had started sleepwalking after our father was taken away for internment.

Fred did not forget his responsibilities and concerns as a father, with frequent advice to Ruth regarding our progress:

16 August

After I'd sent him flowers in the weekly parcel: '*Although somewhat damaged Renée's flowers are very nice and a great joy to me. Can she plant there too?* [I presume he means at the hostel]. *Help her, as it is very useful to be interested in nature.*'

27 August

Send Renée to school. It is better because of languages, English behaviour, etc.'

71

30 August

Renée has round cheeks, but looks at the world with great melancholy. Be very careful with her as she feels everything so deeply, and let her play and romp around as much as possible.'

4 October

'Tell Bobbelchen she must keep an eye on you. The question of schools I leave entirely to you.'

11 October

Later, in response to renewed bombing: *'Don't send Renée to school, to be safe. Maybe find playmates, English children in the neighbourhood.'*

14 October

'Don't force Tommy to eat when he doesn't want to (that is above a certain minimum), while Renée can eat as much as she likes. She'll burn it off again with her fidgeting.'

I can only imagine how my mother felt at receiving some of these instructions!

*　　*　　*

Religious festivals were observed in both camps. From Huyton, Liverpool, Fred mentions that there were prayers and singing for the Jewish New Year at the beginning of October, *'but without me. I pray every day that we can be together soon.'* Christmas on the Isle of Man had a different tone and presaged our future festivities. We always celebrated Christmas, as in Leipzig, with the presents on Christmas Eve, round the tree with candles, which always burned a little of the tree giving that evocative smell of burning pine. I never even knew when the Jewish New Year took place.

After telling Ruth about the cards and little presents he has received and given, he writes:

Did you have a good Xmas? It was quite nice over here. Festive dinner in our house on Christmas Eve (roast pork, roast potatoes and coleslaw), Christmas tree with pretty decorations. On Christmas day hot chocolate and cake (afternoon) together with the Commander and officers at the hotel with a raffle of presents (for me a tin of sardines!) yesterday afternoon 'at my place' in a warm room, porridge with hot chocolate and cake (your brown one and a German Christmas cake everybody in the camp received). Your Stolle has not been started yet and I still hope that we can perhaps do that happily together. By the way we have paid for all improvements and parties, fruit cake etc. out of our own kitty from the canteen and we even invited all our guards with officers to our café yesterday. As you see it wasn't too sad, although the separation from our wives and children was present in all our speeches and our unspoken thoughts as a particularly painful Christmas gift. All the best, my 3 laddies and 1,000 kisses from your Fred.

Fred left the Isle of Man in the spring of 1941. Everyone had to go through a tribunal hearing to assess their suitability for release. His lasted ten minutes. He had established his credentials as a leading surgeon in Leipzig, had gained the respect and friendship of many of the guards at the camp and was declared a friendly alien. He offered his services to the war effort in any way, suggesting the possibility of being an ambulance driver.

My father always told us the story of when Ruth met him on his release, in Manchester, with pride and a certain wryness.

He told her of his offer to become an ambulance driver.

'You can't say you're an ambulance driver! You're a fully qualified surgeon!'

'Well that won't help me now.'

'Nonsense! I want you to see a Professor Burgess here. I heard of him when I was at the Manchester Infirmary, for my gall bladder. He's in charge of the Emergency Services.'

'That's silly. He won't have time for me.'

As usual, Ruth prevailed. Fred went to see Professor Burgess who promptly offered him a surgeon's position under the auspices of the Emergency Medical Services in Macclesfield, in charge of 400 beds. Thus the decision to remain in England for the time being was made for us.

I remember when Fred arrived back at the hostel in Cheadle Hulme. He brought us beautiful toys he had made for us. Mine was a brown and white dog, Tommy's a black and white panda.

Apart from the two visits, we hadn't seen our father for eight months, a long time in a child's calendar. Although I did not understand it at the time, Ruth's dependence on me for comfort, support and, I believe, sometimes advice, must have been a responsibility for a mere five-year-old. What a joy it was to see her so happy and relaxed, to know that that bad time was over and that Fred was home and would look after us all. That was a truly wonderful moment.

On 10 June we moved to Macclesfield, a small town south of Manchester and Fred took up his position in the Parkside Emergency Hospital. The Society of Friends recorded the moment in their minute book:

27 May 1941 Min. 8 Dr Bergmann had been appointed to a medical post in Macclesfield at a salary of £450. He asked for a loan of £25 to cover initial costs of his move. We decided to lend £20 taken from the account lying for his emigration expenses.

28 August 1941 Min. 5 Dr Bergmann had repaid his £20 loan.

6

Macclesfield

The hospital was a magical place. The grounds were vast or so it seemed to me. It was originally what was then called a 'lunatic asylum' and when the Ministry of Defence took it over at the beginning of the war it became a hospital for badly wounded servicemen who needed prolonged treatment such as plastic surgery.

The inmates who suffered mental illness most severely and were considered a danger were rehoused at a distance from the main area and all the others were designated to look after the gardens, the swimming pools and the tennis courts, and run the tuck shop. The visit to the latter was the highlight of my week, when I bought my ration of one Nestlé cream bar. It remains my favourite chocolate, probably for the memories it evokes. I was happy to chat to any adult working in the grounds prepared to listen and I became particularly fond of the small round man who ran the tuck shop.

There were two tennis courts in the grounds. My parents played regularly, and badly, and Tommy and I were equally inept ballboys. But we had great fun and it was all very light-hearted.

Of the two swimming pools, the indoor one we hardly used, preferring the outdoor one. It wasn't actually outdoors but was covered in glass, like an ornate greenhouse. It had a warm, damp, steamy aroma mixed with the smell of chlorine and was quite overgrown with climbing plants, like a jungle, so that when the sun shone, the reflections of leaves and tendrils danced and played on the surface of the water. It was a fairytale place, and we seemed to be the only family that used it. We had our first swimming lessons, in a harness with one or other parent guiding us up and down, issuing instructions. The hospital was rightly named 'Parkside'. It truly was an exotic park, filled with flowering trees and shrubs. For the first time I became aware of the changing seasons, the blossom in the spring and berries in the autumn. Added to this was the novelty of a number of peacocks wandering around. Tommy and I had never seen such glamorous creatures. There was even an aviary, a cage filled with chattering, many-coloured birds.

There was another cage in this paradise. Every fairytale has its dark side – Bluebeard's locked room, the candy house in *Hansel and Gretel*. One day I was taken, inadvertently I'm sure, to the hidden, sad, and to me, terrifying part of Parkside. One of the nurses had offered to look after me for the afternoon. She took me with her to the distant one-storey building where the original patients of the hospital had been rehoused in strict security, and which left me with the impression of caged animals. I did not understand what was happening to these people, dressed in shapeless gowns, with ragged hair, some muttering to themselves endlessly, others shouting and screaming at no one in particular or sitting hunched up on the floor staring into space. I was too frightened to cry or run and was led back, by the nurse, to the main building. The scene, like a Brueghel painting, remains engraved in my mind. When my mother found out where I had been she was incredulous and the unfortunate, but irresponsible nurse felt the full force of Ruth's rage vented on her in all the invective her still hesitant English could muster!

We rented a small upstairs flat on our arrival at Macclesfield. My mother was impressed by our young landlady, who worked full time and could produce an evening meal for herself and her husband in about twenty minutes. For Ruth this was a revelation; she was a great cook, but preparing a meal was a major operation entailing the use of every tool and gadget, resulting in the kitchen looking like a bomb-site. She never changed.

At the recommendation of colleagues at the hospital Tom and I were sent to a private nursery school in a large Victorian house not far from the gates at the rear of the hospital grounds. The fact that this was a Catholic school did not seem to concern our parents. Several times a day we passed the rosary beads through our little fingers with no idea what this represented. Having only just become quite proficient in the English language we learnt Spanish and French with no idea of which was which. Our teachers were two elderly spinster sisters, tall, gaunt and grey, whose main purpose was to instill the fear of hell's fire in us. They succeeded with Tommy. He began to have nightmares and resumed his sleepwalking. I often spent parts of the day banished to 'the corner' to 'tell' my rosary, in disgrace. On one occasion another girl shouted, 'You horrible little Jewish girl.' Quick as a flash I retorted, 'You horrible little Catholic girl.' I spent the rest of the day on my knees in 'the corner'.

We were afraid of our teachers. They locked the large, heavy front door every morning and Tommy and I were sometimes late. We were too scared to knock and would sit miserably in a nearby park until the door was unlocked at break-time. Fred used to take us most of the way to school in the morning. He would walk with us to the hospital gates and leave us to go the short remaining distance on our own. I did not dare tell him of these episodes. I was always nervous and afraid, feeling responsible for my little brother.

They were also unaware of my other activities. I'm not sure how long my particular phobia lasted but I remember the form it took. Ruth and Fred began to have a bit of a social life at the hospital. There were parties, the occasional dance, regular film shows and other entertainments for the soldiers. On the rare evenings they went out we were put to bed and left alone. Baby-sitting regulations were not in force then, and perhaps there was some arrangement with our landlady, but she never came upstairs. As soon as the front door shut I would get out of bed and watch them walk up the road and disappear round the corner. I would then get Tommy up, dress him, dress myself and we would spend the evening sitting (he, poor boy, probably nodding off) by the front bedroom window. There was a blackout and the street was very dark. There was hardly a soul around in this quiet cul-de-sac, but I had to stay alert. As soon as I saw my parent's little flashlight turn the corner, Tommy's clothes were pulled off, I'd undress and we would be back in bed as the key turned in the lock. Why did I do this? I have often asked myself. I can only think that it was an attempt to be prepared for trouble. Although my parents had done everything possible to protect us, the accumulation of fear, the insecurity inherent in the constant change of living space, and, though I never consciously felt it, the continuous threat of imminent danger must have culminated in this strange nocturnal behaviour.

Tommy never made a fuss or queried this procedure (he was only four), nor did he mention it to our parents, but, sweet natured as he was, accepted that I must know best. We were good mates when we were growing up and apart from a more distant time in

Sara Bergmann.

Lazarus Bergmann.

Gebruder Bergmann
department store, Leipzig.

Oma and Opa Bergmann.

Sisters - from left to right, Edith, Claire, Ruth, Leni.

Ruth with Leni (left) and admirers.

Oma and Opa Frankenburg with grandchildren. In front right Leni holding Michelle and Hannelore. Opa holding Maggy. In front Ruth with her whippet dog.

Ruth.

Fred.

Ruth and Fred, playing in the sea before their marriage.

Ruth and Fred in the hospital grounds, Leipzig 1939.

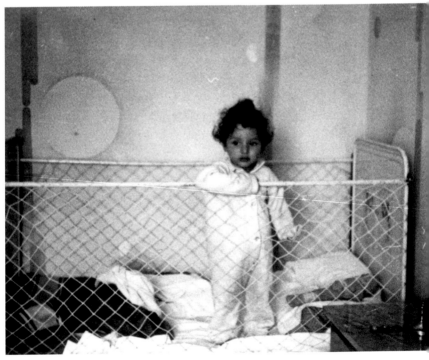

Me in our apartment in Leipzig (Sedanstrasse 17A).

Tommy in Leipzig.

Me in Leipzig aged 2.

Oma and Opa with me
and teddy, Leipzig.

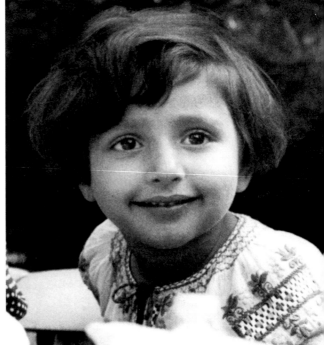

Me in 1938.

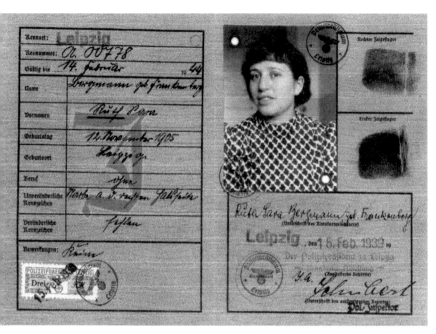

Ruth and Fred's identity cards with the names Sara and Israel.

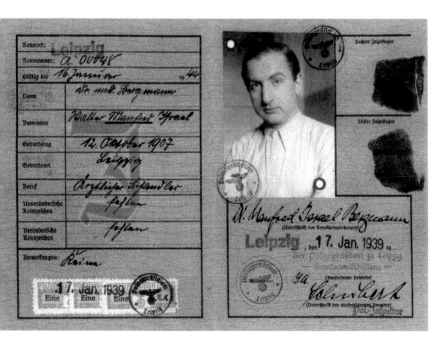

Ilse, Tommy and me in hospital grounds 1939.
(from the book 'We were your Neighbours').

Family group, 1939.

Ruth, Tommy and me on Mrs Brown's lawn, Marple.

Marple primary school. Me, third from right, front row. Mrs Hutton last on right, front row.

Tommy and me in Macclesfield.

Our grey Rover car, in front Bambi, my dog.

First holiday in Anglesey 1945.

Southport, where Fred worked in 1946/47.

Leni in Nahariya.

Claire in Paris, 1952.

Montmorency, France 1946.

The Jewish hospital with the restored Star of David, Leipzig 2006.

Our apartment, 17A Sedanstrasse, Leipzig, 1st floor, 2006.

17A Sedanstrasse, the stairs where Ruth delayed the Gestapo, with her pram, 200(

House in Wanstead.

Lake opposite house.

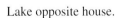

our early marriages have remained so despite the thousands of miles that separate us (he lives in Memphis). We have become even closer in recent years. When we were little Tommy played dolls with me. There were few toys to be had at that time, all the factories having been turned to munitions, but Ruth found two old dolls for us. The bigger one had a stuffed body and a china head, the smaller one was a black baby doll. In Leipzig I had a beautiful big baby doll given to me as a reward for being good when I had my adenoids out in early August 1939, shortly before we left Germany. I remember sitting on the tram as we came home from the surgery and Ruth putting the doll on my lap and I quite forgot that I couldn't swallow! I don't know what happened to my doll, it didn't get to England.

Fred made us a pram from a wooden box and four wheels he found on a rubbish dump. The resulting piercing squeaks from this treasured vehicle announced our whereabouts for miles around. Tommy and I shared a bedroom until I was fourteen and a half and as we got older played general knowledge games at night, such as knowing capital cities. We would start with ten points each and if you didn't know the answer you lost a point. A great way of getting to sleep.

One night, while we were still in the flat, our parents had gone out when Tommy complained of stomachache. I was seven and I was scared. I went downstairs to the miniscule hall, and telephoned the hospital.

'I want to speak to someone in the theatre, please.'

Miraculously I was put through.

'Theatre sister speaking.'

'Hello. My brother has appendicitis. I think he needs an operation. Please get the theatre ready.'

'Who is this?'

'Oh! It's Renée, my daddy is there, Dr Bergmann.'

'Alright, Renée. I'll find your daddy. Don't worry.'

Fred and Ruth were dancing when they were told, 'Your daughter just phoned to ask us to prepare the theatre for an emergency appendectomy on your son.'

You can imagine the speed with which they returned home. Tommy had indigestion! He has continually reminded me that, before this was diagnosed, he was subjected to an enema. He has not forgiven me!

This bizarre episode has its roots in the family neurosis with the appendix. Both Ruth's brothers died in infancy from this condition, one due to bad aftercare, and the other through belated diagnosis. I was brought up with a detailed knowledge of the symptoms.

I had my own appendix removed at the hospital when I was ten. I had a great time. It was June and my room, with French doors, opened on to an overgrown bit of garden, humming with bees amongst the wild flowers in the long grass. Best of all, every soldier who was mobile came to visit me, sit on my bed and tell me stories.

*   *   *

By 1942 we were renting our own little house, 35 Ivy Road, in a quiet residential street with fields at the far end (where, unbeknown to us and our neighbours there also resided an unexploded bomb!) and had our own garden. We would stay there until the end of the war. It became an oasis of calm and security and we began to enjoy a more stable family life. I allowed Tommy to sleep on the nights our parents went out and began my lifelong addiction to reading. As soon as they left for their evening out, on would go the bedside light, and later when I heard the key turn in the door out it would go and my acting career started with innocent, well-feigned sleep. It didn't last long. My father just touched the still very hot light bulb and I was discovered. Their threat, that I would lose the lamp, didn't work: I got the timing wrong and it was confiscated. After that I simply used a torch under the bedclothes.

Fred seemed content with his work at the hospital. I became inured to the gory details of operations related over the supper table and was happy to see him happy. The nurses took more responsibility for post-operative care here than he was used to and he was impressed by their high standard of training and efficiency. My father would tell us with great delight about the animated conversations held by the operating team during surgery about the latest cricket scores, and the playing of music in the theatre. This relaxed attitude contrasted sharply with the more authoritarian, terse atmosphere he had encountered in Germany. He rapidly became known as a good surgeon and Professor Burgess from the Manchester Infirmary began to send him difficult civilian cases and, in time, less urgent ones as Fred initiated greater use of local rather than general anaesthetics.

And Ruth? Well, she settled into a more peaceful, domestic life. She cooked, baked, sewed and looked after us all. She still had sporadic bouts of illness. In April 1945, in the last entry in my book in German, she records something of our life at that time:

Although we got here penniless and all our things, clothes, furniture and household goods stayed in Amsterdam and are certainly lost (we didn't have the money to have them sent here when that was still possible and we have heard that the Germans have confiscated everything), we have been able since Pappi works at an Army Hospital to provide a life for you which differs in nothing from an English child of our social status. Pappi turned part of the garden into a chicken yard, Tommy owns two white cats (mother and son), and you, Bobbilein, got a part shepherd dog for your 9th birthday, named Bambi. The nicest room in the house is the children's bedroom, and you are even having the only good piece to sleep on, a couch, while Pappi and I sleep on a mattress and Tommy on a camp bed. Fred not only built the chicken sheds – we keep on average 12 to 14 hens – but also the furniture for the sitting room out of storage crates from the local shop. Thanks to my, if limited, skills in sewing the two of you are always dressed nicely, and when Pappi got himself a car recently you asked, 'Now we are no longer poor, aren't we in fact rich now?' That we are not, although we live very economically, but saving so far has not led to big sums! We have absolutely nothing of any value, not even a piece of furniture we could take with us one day, and it wont be easy to build a new life.

Of course we do not think ever to return to Germany, and have applied already almost a year ago for naturalisation, when we had been here for just 5 years. During the war they don't issue them but we hope it will happen soon. Pappi was not allowed to take his exam although he is in the position of a leading surgeon (not at all being paid as such) and we don't know therefore what the future will be like. Will we be able to stay here? Will they let Pappi work as a surgeon? How great and numerous will be the difficulties they will create for him?

Although our parents made every effort to conceal from us their considerable worries about their family and friends, and their distress as the news about what was happening to the Jews in Europe began to seep through, we sensed their fears. For me it was just a continuation of what I had become used to. I do remember that occasionally they listened to broadcasts in German, maybe Radio Free Europe. I was warned never to mention this to anyone so when I forgot and they heard me shout to an enquiring neighbour in the garden, 'They're busy. They're listening to the German wireless,' I was soundly smacked and sent to my room. I have no idea what station my parents were tuning into and can only assume that they were searching for news of relatives.

It didn't take long for Ruth and Fred to become aware of the damage St Teresa's school was inflicting on us when they realised Tommy's nightmares were caused by his fear of burning alive in hell and it was discovered that we were locked out when we were late, probably in a report from the school. We were removed to the local state primary school, which had neither the wonderment and love of my first school in Marple, nor the fear and hostility of the second.

On my father's rare days off we would take the local train to Buxton. These were exciting, special days. We would walk across fields, clamber over stiles, searching for the perfect spot for our picnic and I never got tired. Once I fell into a large, fresh cow pat and I remember our embarrassment on the train coming home with my stained, brown-streaked clothing.

Memory is a strange phenomenon. Why do some instances remain clear and others a blank? Do we forget the inconsequential details but also the important moments we don't wish to remember? What triggers the selection? I remember so little about Leipzig and that first year in England while my father was interned. Yet

Tommy, three years younger, remembers clearly his black and white panda. Later, his recollections of Kilburn are sharper than mine, when again Fred was absent and times were hard. On reflection, my memories are often about embarrassment and shame (the cow pat, for instance).

During, and for some time after the war, clothing was strictly rationed. Imagine then my mother's delight to have enough coupons and be able to afford a new tweed coat for me. It was simple, well-fitting, in unobtrusive tweedy colours and warm; in short a perfect find! And yet I remember so well the misery it caused me. The coat buttoned the wrong way! It was a boy's coat. I became the butt of much teasing and hilarity amongst my peers. Standing at the bus-stop waiting for the school bus became a different sort of humiliation from the hostile spitting in Leipzig.

Ruth did wonders with our rations or rather, as she put it, 'I've come for my russians,' much to the amusement of the local shopkeepers. She vehemently refused any offers on the black market and to the end of her life disapproved of any deviance from the law, however slight. She made the most of what she had legitimately. As we never used our entire sugar ration she exchanged this for boiled sweets and these were kept for special days out and our holiday. Hexagonal, octagonal, triangular, zebra-striped, pastel pink, green, lilac, mouth-watering, gob-stopping sweets were kept in a large glass jar. She made delicious stews with 'lights' (offal) in a mustard sauce and most of our tea ration (my parents were more accustomed to drinking coffee) she gave to friends and neighbours. Fred took up a new enthusiasm, keeping chickens, so we always had plenty of eggs. They were free ranging in our little garden with a cock that crowed and was mercifully accepted by the neighbours. They had other concerns at the time such as the unexploded bomb at the end of the road, which once discovered took some time to be considered safe. As he became more proficient, Fred began to hatch our own chicks. Tommy and I were enchanted, listening to the feeble peck pecking of the new life and watching the gradual cracking of the fragile shell as the tiny damp chicks emerged under the special lamp installed in the box room. As they became fully grown they had rings attached to their legs, each with their own colour combination, so we knew them individually. We were thankfully excluded from the more distasteful aspects such as killing the birds and then plucking them. My favourite one was the 'red and white'. She became quite a pet. One Sunday lunch the roast was put on the table.

'Which one is this?' I asked casually.

'The red and white,' came the answer. I rushed from the table in tears. I couldn't eat *her*. Much later we kept chickens again, but by that time it was so automated, they were more confined, and all the fun was gone.

Sunday lunch was very special. Sometimes the grocer would have tinned pears. Fred would dish these out with due solemnity, and we would eat our portion slowly, savouring each mouthful. After lunch we would sit around the wireless and listen to the BBC Home Service's classic serial at 3 p.m. This was my introduction to Tolstoy, Dostoevsky and Dickens. We listened to *War and Peace* every Sunday for weeks. Then came *Anna Karenina*. I owe my love of reading, particularly Russian and French classics, to my mother. She encouraged me from an early age and the dramatisations on the wireless were a wonderful stimulus. By the age of twelve I had read most of Dickens and for the first of many times subsequently *War and Peace*. How I loved the romance of Natasha and Andre and Pierre and how little I understood then of the philosophy and politics.

Another rare treat was a visit to the cinema. We always politely refused Fred's offer of an ice cream, because we knew he couldn't afford cinema *and* ice cream. There was a Shirley Temple film, which I remember as all fire, a screen filled with flames and it frightened me so much that I had to sleep in my parents' bed for several nights afterwards; and Walt Disney's *Bambi* and *Dumbo* left me red-eyed with weeping. Perhaps an ice cream and no film would have been preferable.

We established future patterns of behaviour. Coming home from school, leaning against the kitchen door frame, coat and beret still on, satchel dangling from my shoulder, the habit of years began as I regaled my mother with a blow by blow account of my day.

'Mummy, you're not listening! Are you listening?' I would nag her as she bustled around the tiny kitchen preparing our tea.

'Yes, yes I'm listening,' she'd say without taking her eyes off the saucepan on the rusty old enamel cooker.

This was also the beginning of the legendary 'dainty dishes', so named by Fred for the cakes that didn't rise, the misshapen biscuits, and other culinary disasters created by Ruth. But they always tasted fine, and Fred's 'Ah! Another dainty dish!' caused endless amusement to us children.

Our parents, not surprisingly, were (and remained) over protective of Tommy and me. We were not allowed to have bicycles ... too dangerous! I was 57 when my mother insisted on paying for my first bike. My friend Daphne lived on our street in Macclesfield. She had long, thick brown plaits, and she had a bike. Whenever my parents were out of the way I practised and then rode up and down the road with much enjoyment. There was enough gradient to give the downhill ride a precarious thrill. In 1944 we acquired an old silver-grey Rover, a luxurious classic car with the unforgettable opulent smell of an all-leather interior. One day I was freewheeling happily downhill, the wind in my hair, when the Rover hove into sight, coming straight towards me. I don't know who was the most shocked, my parents or me! I fell off the bike and I still have the scar on my knee.

Before we left Macclesfield there were two episodes that brought painful echoes from the past, one I was told about, the other I experienced. As the war drew to a close truckloads of German prisoners appeared at the hospital, needing medical and surgical treatment. My father, true to his Hippocratic oath, performed operations on them as he had on all the soldiers in his care. The hospital had two towers on site servicing the incinerators. Fred was amazed to see some of the prisoners, on seeing the smoke coming from the towers, throw themselves on the ground, begging for mercy. They thought they had been taken to gas chambers. My father was shocked and surprised to think that ordinary soldiers in the German Army knew of the concentration camps with their gas chambers in Germany and Eastern Europe. What was not known at that time was that in the dying days of the war, as the allies advanced, many of the SS guards, to save themselves, had fled the concentration camps and melted into the army. Could these men have been amongst the ones my father witnessed, men who would recognise those towers?

Opposite our house, a little further down the road, was a piece of derelict ground designated for the building of two police houses. German prisoners of war were drafted in to begin the building work. I passed the site on my way to school. I remember my utter surprise, followed by prickles of remembered fear, as they called after me, *Kleine Juden.*

In 1945 we had our first holiday, in Anglesey. We stayed on a farm and we went for long walks on the beaches, breathing in the salty, clean air, talking and talking endlessly about our future, how important it was for us to work hard, to pass the eleven plus exam to ensure entrance to a good school. Ruth and Fred discussed their plans: how he would need to take exams too in order to get English qualifications; and what about naturalisation, if we decided to stay here, should we change our name? Neither wanted to keep a German name. What would be the job prospects for Fred when all the surgeons now serving on the front came home? He had a reputation as an innovative and excellent surgeon in Manchester. Would that guarantee a permanent surgeon's position? If we moved to London would finding work be more difficult? The milder climate for Ruth's health and my aspirations to go on the stage were two of the reasons given for the move south.

The questions ebbed and flowed back and forth as did the sea on the sands we were walking along. But my most vivid memory of that holiday was not of the beautiful beaches, the newfound freedom of having a car, the experience of farm animals seen at close quarters. No, what I remember is my darling mother painting her nails bright, shiny red. It was the first time in my life I had seen her do this and for me it epitomised a new era, one of luxury and leisure. How wrong I was proved to be.

7

Moving South to Kilburn

Why did we leave the north and move to London? My father had gained an enviable reputation as a skilled surgeon and an innovator in the use of local anaesthetics. The letters of reference from Professors Morley and Burgess from the Manchester Infirmary sang his praises both as a brilliant professional and as a colleague. So why start all over again in a new environment? The answers I was given as a child were that the educational opportunities were greater in London; the climate was drier and warmer, beneficial to Ruth's health. And I think now that they wanted to be at the heart of things. Coming from another country London would be an ambition fulfilled. But what we gained in weather warmth we lost in human warmth. No more 'Alright, luv?' 'Ticket please, luv.' 'See you again, luv.' The cocoon of warm northern 'luv' in a small town was lost in the more impersonal coldness of London, and I missed it.

We went to live at 15 Priory Road, Kilburn. A distant cousin of my father's, who had recently moved out of the district, found the house for us. It was a three-storey Edwardian semi-detached town house set back from the street by a small garden, and we rented the first and second floors. The front had a large, elegant bay window topped by two rectangular bedroom windows. I went back to find the house recently, and rather nervously trespassed down the side passage to see if I could get a glimpse of the garden. I remember it as high banked from the basement, with trees at the back, the washing line stretching across and the corrugated steel air raid shelter at the back. The family in the basement were called Sullivan.

A woman came out of the basement entrance, dustpan and brush in hand, presumably to tidy away the autumn leaves.

'I'm sorry, I hope you don't mind, I used to live here, a long time ago, after the war.'

'Oh yes, what was your name then?' she asked. It transpired that she was born in 1946 and had lived in that basement all her life, so it was her parents I had chatted to when I went to play in the garden, or hang out the washing. But I can't recall a baby at all.

Priory Road has now the ambience of a leafy, well-to-do London suburb, and Kilburn High Road bears no resemblance, with its flashy boutiques, multiple convenience stores and sophisticated international food, to what I recall back then: the bakers, the draper with peach-coloured bras, long johns, jumbled with rainbow balls of wool, hosiery, caps and gloves in the window; the one chemist; the grocers, selling everything from boot polish to tins of spam, with slabs of butter and cheese on the open counter. There were the butchers selling only horsemeat. I used to be sent to buy slices of the lean, pink, sweetish-tasting meat ostensibly for pets, but probably supplementing many other families' meat ration. Along the pavement on the High Road the barrow boys would wheel up their (to us) exotic fruits, shouting encouragement to buy: 'Come on, lady, lovely tomatoes, only 'alf a penny a pound!' All around were the bomb-damaged buildings, the obsolete shelters, stinking, full of rubbish and worse. These were the playgrounds for the local children.

Our part of the house was in a sad state of neglect. I was responsible for cleaning the existing cracked linoleum in the bathroom and on the stairs, and we covered the rest of the floors with roofing felt.

My big little daughter has been a great deal of help during her last holidays. I was not feeling so well and you took over looking after the floors and promised to do so as long as we cannot get any help. You are a thorough and good cleaner, but I don't like your working so hard at your age and as peace seems very near there will be somebody I hope to relieve you of this hard work. I pay you for your 'services' and you are saving hard for a bycicle [sic] and your Christmas gift you send every year for poor children who are in the care of the Quakers, the people whose wonderful help saved our lives – a fact you must never forget, we constantly bring this to your attention.

Tommy and I had the largest room. They made it nice for us and Ruth was pleased with the result. It was April 1945 and her first entry in English.

You and Tommy have again the largest bedroom all cream coloured with green eiderdowns and pretty coloured curtains. You are very proud of it and keep it extremely clean and tidy, but not the drawers ... (but who am I to judge? To be read in 20 years time!).

Ruth had her individual style of tidiness. She was in fact very untidy. Having been brought up with servants she was not used to doing the job herself. At the same time she was very house-proud,

93

so when we had visitors all the rooms had to be cleaned regardless of whether visitors would see anything other than the living-room. She dealt with the chaos, particularly in her bedroom by stuffing everything willy-nilly into cupboards and drawers.

The next two years were full of changes and contradictions. Life was hard for my parents, but they did their best to protect us. Given the time and the circumstances it was hard for most people, adjusting to a peace, which still had rationing, the massive rebuilding and so much loss. In my childish dreams peace meant bananas. I was convinced that the day peace was declared there would be bananas in all the greengrocers. I was disappointed, and so were millions of others when the peace did not mean an instant relief from wartime restrictions.

Tommy and I were sent to the local primary school. One day we were waiting in the dinner queue out in the yard when the school bully came up to me and pushed me out of the line. Tommy was close behind me. He marched up to the much bigger boy (Tommy was eight years old and small for his age):

'Leave my sister alone!' he yelled and promptly had his two front teeth knocked out!

Even worse was to have to tell our mother on the phone from the headmaster's office.

'Please don't cry, Mummy. It's only two teeth, please don't cry!'

The headmaster, Mr Hadida, was a charming, kindly man who both liked and was liked by our parents (he coached Tommy for the eleven plus exam). It was a rough environment and he was not opposed to using the cane. Being small and slight, perhaps to add some weight to the punishment he would give a little jump as he struck the offending pupil's palm, a mannerism that caused much amusement to the rest of the class. He had to retire early due to damage to his eyes inflicted by a pupil. Inner-city school violence is not a late twentieth-century development. There were just no TV cameras to report the attack on Mr Hadida.

Our strong Lancashire dialect made us the butt of teasing at the best, bullying at the worst, so we very quickly adopted the London/Kilburn dialect. My stay at the school was mercifully brief, as I had passed the eleven plus and entered Parliament Hill School in Highgate in September 1946.

The overriding element of this period was our lack of an income. The sale of our Rover car for £80 had paid for our move to London but most of that had now been spent. It became clear that Fred's German MD qualification needed to be converted to the British MRCS. As the war ended surgeons operating at the fronts returned home and the doors to future employment closed. Fred was advised by one consultant to marry a consultant's daughter. 'That's the best way into the profession, old chap.'

As he had no previous qualifications in this country, Fred had to get special permission from the Royal College of Surgeons to be able to sit the exams, thus the importance of the references. He set himself the task, normally spanning seven years of study, of passing in just one year. He succeeded, except for the last exam, which much to his chagrin, he had to retake. Time was not on his side with a wife and two children to feed, there was no unemployment or any other benefit or grant, and the exams cost money. His routine was to study all day, closeted in the front room, surrounded by enormous, heavy leather-bound text books from the British Medical Reference Library, and on the stroke of midnight he would take my dog, Bambi, and walk around the silent, empty streets, then home and bed.

Poor Bambi! My beautiful black and white dog, who liked to

95

chase cows on our walks through the fields in Macclesfield, and who at one time put us in danger of being sued by an angry farmer. When we moved to London he ran away frequently and in the end the police advised us to have him put down. Sadly, he was a country dog and just couldn't cope with life in Kilburn.

*   *   *

From the summer of 1946 to March 1947 Fred moved to Southport, working as a surgeon in the Emergency Hospital and continuing his studies at the same time. He wrote to Ruth almost every day and most of his letters have survived, although hardly any of Ruth's, but one can surmise some of their content from his replies. The letters build a picture of a loving, at times tumultuous relationship, bearing another separation reluctantly. They are tender love letters and illuminate Fred's personality poignantly. Occasionally he was granted a weekend leave and his Monday letters paint a vivid picture of how much those two precious days meant and also the friction between them.

> *I am so glad that you were as happy as I was being together again. It was a really 'perfect' week-end and I am very much looking forward to the next one. I shall officially notice then the Henna during the first hour and not mention it only at the very last minute. But you must have noticed that I repeatedly told you how nice your hair looks and that included colour as well! I think it is all the better that your hair has that natural Henna tint and does not look 'dyed' and conspicuous.*

And one wonders what occurred on another weekend!

My dearest, dearest Lumpchen,

You are a silly little thing and I am sorry that I gave you the impression that I don't like you to be a fighter. I did approve of it as you are right to fight for a happy and decent home. If you would not be a fighter we would not be here! You misunderstood me and I really hope you will always be a fighter (though not with me as the victim!).

On another occasion he ends with: '*Quite a lot of "unrestrained" kisses for my little (very little indeed) thunderstorm.*'

Much of the content of the letters is taken up, as it did from internment, with his anxiety for Ruth, her health and welfare. His constant admonitions are not to work so hard, to rest, eat generously, especially fresh fruit (which we had largely been denied during the war years) and to keep warm.

'*Don't be greedy with the heater* [he meant 'sparing', I think] *as electricity is even relatively cheaper than gas. Use 2,000 watts and have it warm! And that's an order!*'

Fred pays all the bills from Southport and sends her detailed accounts, delighted that gas and electricity are cheaper than he expected, plus details of his bank account, encouraging her not to be mean and to spend enough for our comfort.

He finds working and studying hard going. From a letter dated 3 January 1947:

I had rather [sic] *busy 24 hours since yesterday morning (3 operations) and after reading until 11 another op (accident) so that I went to bed at 2 instead of 11 as I intended.*

And again on 13 January:

There is nothing wrong here but we have more work to do now and I regret every minute I can't work for the exam. If it would not have been for the money I would not have gone to S. at all, you can be sure. And what is wrong is the long distance from here to you and that was wrong from the beginning.

The worries for the future persist. He is applying for jobs everywhere. A resident senior surgeon's position is discussed at £900–£1,200 p.a. He thinks we might get a house nearby, and he would not need to be on duty all the time. But he is depressed at the prospects. *'I'm afraid that the FRCS and ex-servicemen will first be absorbed before I have a chance.'* And the question of emigrating to the USA is still being discussed.

I think you are right we should try to become English and if I should get on to the permanent register – which I very much doubt without exam – then we have always something to go back to, and have something in case U.S.A. does not realise at all. On the whole I am in favour of U.S.A. as I don't see much future for our children here. Many young English people emigrate because this country will be poor for many years, and might remain so for ever if they don't change considerably.

Knowing my parents' love of and staunch loyalty to this country I find these sentiments surprising, but given the circumstances, the worry and stress they were under to build a viable future, I can understand.

On a lighter note, no longer able to play football, Fred takes up the pools. I wonder how interested Ruth was in the details!

*My football pool was wrong again and it was very bad luck!
Out of 13 I got 10 right and you win for 13, 12 or 11 right.
Just one missed. But still it is not as bad as missing the 3 of
you. Will you be sensible and not work yourself to pieces
before I come home? I like some mess, and some dirt, and
before all I like a smiling, well slept, good and young looking
girlfriend as my wife, seeee?*

Last weeks [sic] *football pools went wrong again. The last
dividend is for 16 points. I got 15! So you will have to wait
with all the jewels, fur coats, maids, etc ... for another week!*

He enjoyed listening to the same radio programmes as Ruth, it
was one way of being close, and there are references to such old
favourites as *Much Binding in the Marsh* and *Twenty Questions*.
One letter is to Tommy and me: *'Keep upright, Renée!'* refers to
my stooping posture. There are frequent mentions of food
shortages and ration books: *'I wanted to send some chocolate for
the children but couldn't get any.'*

I had been given a little old gramophone and I remember when
he gave Ruth The Ink Spots' record of 'Bless You for Being an
Angel' and how she played it over and over again whenever she
had the time.

My dearest Lumpchen,
*Bless you, I meant it, and I mean it and I shall always mean it
(that is as long as you remain that silly, little sweet bit you
are). That's that. And don't be touched now and think, 'how
sweet he is'. I was just looking round for a signature tune, or
better my signature tune and chose it, sentimental ass as I
am, living on 'Einbildung' and dreams.*

We joined Fred for our summer holiday, staying in a boarding house he had found for us. The landlady remains a nebulous image, but her collection of the entire works of Charles Dickens, bound in green and gold, is a vivid one. I worked my way through this treasure trove, weeping at the death of Dora, and Steerforth's drowning in *David Copperfield*; bereft at the fate of Little Nell; mesmerised by the mystery of *Bleak House* and quite overcome by the noble and tragic end to *The Tale of Two Cities*. I finally fell foul of our landlady's wrath when she discovered that I was taking her precious books to the beach. After that I read by torchlight under the bed covers.

When not reading, I had to accompany my cousin Maggy, who was on a visit from Paris, to the beach, together with a young man, Horst. He and another teenager, Helmut, had come over with the Kindertransport at the beginning of the war, landed in Macclesfield and been befriended by Ruth. There they had regularly come for Sunday lunch. Helmut, tall and blond, eventually went to America. He used to throw Tommy up in the air and always made him cry! Horst, short and dark, became a professional singer, but at this time he had joined us for a week in Southport. He and Maggy would giggle and wriggle under a blanket on the beach. I had no idea what they were doing but whatever it was I felt left out and bored so I would rhythmically throw a ball at the undulating rug, jump on it, tug at it, in short, do my best to be a nuisance and stop their fun.

* * *

It was Ruth at this time who initially provided and then supplemented the income. She took cleaning jobs, she sewed bags out of strips of canvas, which she dyed different bright colours to sell, and she took in lodgers. One day she remarked on a man she had just let a room to. 'It's funny, he hasn't got any luggage, not even a bag. Maybe his toothbrush is in his pocket!' Two days later he disappeared. Then we saw the headlines and the picture in the *Evening Star*. His name (not the one he gave us) was Haigh; he was a wanted murderer on the run. After that Ruth became more cautious in her choice of lodger. One was a former conductor and composer, who started me on piano lessons, and Tommy had violin lessons with a music student from Palestine, Erich Gruenberg. He was to become one of Britain's most distinguished violinists, and to receive an OBE. Neither charged for their tutelage and, sadly, we did not appreciate the privilege at the time, and were not willing to practise seriously.

Ruth paid me for the jobs I did around the house, so I had some pocket money but when I knew she was short and worried about the next meal I would slip the few coins into her purse. I was very pleased with my subterfuge and it wasn't until after her death in 1993 when I found her book that I realised that she knew what I had done and she was touched.

To this day I don't know how she managed so well on so little. When I had friends from school to tea there was always a good spread. Plates of little bright yellow cakes with technicolour pink, green and red icing on top, and always a warm welcome. I was embarrassed by the amount and the hospitality and compared it to my best friend, who lived in a beautiful house on Hampstead Heath (Gerald Du Maurier's old home). When we went to tea, her mother was never there and we would raid the larder for anything consumable. How I envied her freedom and how she possibly envied me for the mother always there and the tea laid out. We were never really hungry, but sometimes a second helping would have been nice. However, the fledgling Welfare State ensured that we had free milk at break time (which I hated!) and subsidised school dinners (which I loved!). Here I was introduced to puddings I had not had before: spotted dick; roly-poly; chocolate sponge; treacle tart, all generously covered with lumpy custard. Heaven!

*　　*　　*

On 16 September 1946 we were granted British nationality. We also changed our name. Bergmann was not exclusively German. Both the Swedes, actress Ingrid and director Ingmar (Bergman with a single 'n') were stars at the time. I accepted the change unquestioningly, as anxious as my parents to melt into anonymity and be the same as my schoolmates. I frequently reproached them for speaking German to each other at home. Tommy and I spoke only English, it was his first language and I had consciously forgotten my German. Ruth and Fred reverted to it in moments of stress, usually when they quarrelled. They rapidly learnt to speak very good English. Fred was sometimes mistaken for a Scotsman, much to his delight. He was quick to pick up colloquialisms and used 'By jove!' often and with relish! Ruth retained a slight accent (she spoke German with a strong Saxony dialect much softer than Hochdeutsch), which I didn't notice through long habit. But my friends always knew when I spoke to her on the phone as they assured me, to my dismay, that I immediately acquired a German accent.

While Fred was in Southport the practicalities of a name change were discussed. Ruth writes:

I enclose a letter of Mrs Budenberg. I think she is right and we shall choose a name from the directionary [sic]. *I shall ask her about Hillman or with one 'L' as the correct translation. What do you think?*

102

Fred replies:

About our name, we shall look for a nice one. What about Churchill or Attlee????? Why Hillman with one L? Is our 'Berg' so small? Or are you so used to economise that you would not spend a second 'L'?

They did pick a name from the telephone directory. It was decided that it had to start with a 'B' (to keep initials the same) and needed to be an infrequent entry. The thinking behind this was that future patients could find him speedily, so ploughing through hundreds of 'Browns', for example, would not do. They came up with 'Brent' (American origin, I think). Unimaginative, boring, but I must tread carefully. My brother and his two sons Matt and Tim, bear the name, and a baby girl, born July 2003 to one of my nephews, has been named Ruth, so another Ruth Brent is with us. Hallelujah!

The change of name had one amusing side effect. Ruth wrote to my school to give them the information and I sensed increased warmth, sympathetic glances and a greater leniency to my undoubted laziness from the Head downwards. It wasn't until the next parents' evening that Ruth explained to an embarrassed tutor that no, he was my real father, no, she had not divorced and remarried, and after that the gentle approach swiftly evaporated.

There have been massive social changes in the last 50 to 60 years, not least the growth and acknowledgement of a multi-cultural society. Now refugees and immigrants are expected to retain their culture and traditions. But in 1939 my family came to a country at war, from the enemy country. Ruth and Fred did not want any association with their German past, thus Bergmann had to go.

I don't know exactly when I began the slow process of questioning my parents' actions. I fully understand and respect their motives. Ruth and Fred wanted to feel safe, to disappear into the great ocean of Englishness, never to be singled out again. I regret that in the process we lost some of our traditions, such as the family gathering on Friday nights, and the festivals, and could no longer pass them on to the next generation. We celebrate Christmas and Easter, that's fine, but why not Hanukkah and Yom Kippur too?

For many years I had my own identity dilemma. People were always asking me: 'Where d'you come from?'

'Macclesfield.'

'Where?'

'Near Manchester.'

'But you don't look English.'

Now here I could say I was born in Germany, but then I would need to qualify that with, 'But I'm Jewish.' The years of denial through necessity and fear clung on, like a bad smell. Then I had an idea. My first name was the answer.

'Well actually I'm French. I have an aunt who lives in Paris on the Champs-Elysées.' Problem solved. It wasn't until my first visit to Israel with my youngest son, Sebastian, in 1986 that I felt an overwhelming sense of relief – of coming home. No one queried who I was and where I came from. They just knew.

*　　*　　*

In spite of the general greyness of that time, we had our starry moments. One was the sudden appearance of Kurt Weill to waft Ruth, like Cinderella, to the first night of *Annie Get Your Gun*. The other memorable events were the reunion with her adored

104

surviving sisters, Claire and Leni. For me this was the first time I became conscious that we had 'family' other than the four of us. Of course Ruth had talked a great deal about her sisters and how devoted they had always been, but now they became real. And I was jealous. Ruth and I were very close, real companions, partly due to circumstances. She had few acquaintances and no real friends. Coming from a very active social background in Leipzig and Berlin, with many friends from her childhood, she never regained her openness and trust in people, and she often asked for my advice and shared problems. So it came as a shock when suddenly there appeared two strangers who took all her attention, and even more disturbing, treated her as the little sister, telling her what to do and generally being bossy. One instance that affected me directly was my weekend lie-in. Ruth encouraged me to sleep as long as I wished, or read in bed, sometimes until midday on Saturday and Sunday, believing that as I worked hard and long all week I deserved this lassitude. Her sisters strongly advised her to change such a bad habit. 'She'll end up lazy and slovenly!'

They all used the affectionate term 'maus', so it was Ruthimaus, Clairemaus, and Lenimaus. Quite nauseating, I thought. As for Fred, they all three treated him as if he were the last male on earth! However, given the state of both my aunts' marriages, as I understood later, this was not surprising.

They were wonderful and sad women and deserve a chapter of their own.

8

Claire

She descended on grey, drab Kilburn in 1946 like a bird of paradise into a chicken coup.

Known as the 'beautiful Claire' in her youth in Leipzig, it was said that artists queued up to paint or photograph her, and her legs were compared to those of the film star Betty Grable (the latter's being insured for a vast amount of money).

The oldest of the four sisters, she trained and worked as a dressmaker until she married Vivid Levy, a wealthy coalmine owner. They had left Germany in 1933 with their two daughters, Michelle (eight years old), Maggy (four), and settled in France, and that was where they were when the French capitulated to the German Army. They spent the occupation years on the run. My cousins have since told me how they jumped out of back windows as the German soldiers or the Gestapo broke down the front door. They were constantly on the move, afraid to trust anyone. Joining the French Resistance movement and working for them probably saved their lives. On one of their hurried escapes, Claire broke both her legs and because of the lack of proper medical care and having to keep moving on they healed badly, so when I met her the legendary legs were sadly no more. She never talked about that episode; I heard it from Ruth, so maybe it paled into insignificance compared to the survival of her husband and children. However, they did not escape from tragedy. Towards the end of 1944 Michelle, just 19, met, fell in love with and married a fellow resistance worker. They had a baby girl, Cathy. When she was only a few months old the retreating German Army caught her father and shot him. It was just days before the cease-fire was declared.

In 1945 much of Europe lay in ruins. It was the time for men of enterprise and vision and my uncle was one of them. An astute man of business, he saw the need for rebuilding and for raw materials. Having lost one fortune, he went into the scrap metal trade and made another.

Claire came to London in 1946 and Ruth met her at Victoria Station off the boat train from Calais. When she walked into our home amid much joy and emotion, I just hope our mouths (Tommy's and mine) were not too open with amazement. She wore a figure-hugging tailored suit (Christian Dior's 'New Look'), in a soft grey material, high-heeled shoes with a bag of the same leather, long pale-grey gloves and a delicate confection in grey and white over one eye. In her ears and around her neck were clusters of minute glass fruits. Her lips were shiny red and her eyelids showed a gentle hint of blue. I had never seen anyone so beautiful. I had never smelt anyone like her before. She moved in an aura of heady, sensual sweetness. That was my first memory of 'Tante' Claire. But after the initial shock of her gorgeous clothes and exotic jewellery, I remember her smile, big, warm and guileless, and her large deep-brown eyes. Aged eleven, I was strangely moved by her smile without knowing why. Later I recognised the sadness in her eyes, but even then I sensed the vulnerability and unhappiness under the layers of chic and *haute couture*.

On all her visits to stay with us Tante Claire always shared my bedroom. We never managed the luxury of a guest room, even in Wanstead. On this first visit Tommy must have moved in with our parents. The bedtime scene was always the same. She would come to bed hours after my bedtime and she would whisper, 'Renée, *tu dors?*'

I would remain still and silent, breathing regularly, feigning sleep. Modesty thus assured Claire would get undressed and I would marvel again and again and delight in watching her peel off the delicate silk underwear; each night a different set of peach, ivory, cream, black or white. To me the ultimate luxury was to have such finery privately next to one's skin and unseen by others. I don't think she ever knew that I watched her with such pleasure. Now I wonder how she must have felt about the very different circumstances her younger sister was in. The euphoria of finding each other, of having survived must have put all other feelings aside. I have to smile at the incongruity of the image of the two of them shopping in Kilburn High Road, the one looking as if she had stepped straight out of the latest *Vogue* magazine (eyebrows must have been raised!), the other in her shabby cast-offs. I knew, just from the look on her face, how much pride and admiration my mother felt for her adored sister. But maybe something in the situation prompted Claire to invite us all, and pay the fare, for a little holiday in France.

* * *

Montmorency is a village about 45 kilometres from Paris. My aunt and uncle lived in the chateau: an elegant old house with multiple windows, conservatories and balconies set in its own grounds with an imposing drive to the front courtyard. At first sight Tommy and I thought it was a grand hotel. It took a little time for us to adjust to the fact that this was a one-family home. We felt we were living in a dream, the house, the grounds and the car. Meals were taken in a grand dining-room with crystal and silver and we all had napkins in our own rings! There was always a large bowl of fruit on the table topped by an enormous bunch of grapes, an unknown luxury at home. All so different, exciting, disconcerting too.

One day Tommy and I were exploring and we found jars of what looked like fruit in a darkish liquid in the long elegant sideboard.

'What's that?' whispered Tommy.

'Don't know. There's labels.'

'What does it say?'

'Don't know. CERISE … PECHE,' I spelled out. 'I think it's French for fruits.'

'Open one!'

'No we can't. They'll find out.'

'Just one,' begged Tommy. 'I want to try.'

I managed to prise the lid off a jar and we stuck our fingers in and sucked.

'Ugh!' said Tommy, pulling a face in disgust. But to me the juice tasted strong and sweet, the fruit soft and rich.

Later when there were guests for dinner the jars were brought out and bowls of the liquored fruits were handed round. We were allowed a taste with a lot of laughter and comments about little fingers having already been there. We didn't get into trouble but I wondered at the time, why did they assume it was us?

Our cousins Maggy and Michelle were very French and to me intriguingly different. They wore slacks or short pleated skirts with bobby socks and tight-fitting sweaters. I remember one worn by Michelle, all stripes of bright colours, red, green, yellow and purple. I thought they were both wonderfully glamorous. Cathy was still a baby and appeared to be looked after by everyone, but mostly Claire. Michelle was working for Uncle Vivid and seemed too young and pretty to be a mother. Maggy was an art student with a large portfolio full of nudes, which made her even more fascinating. They were both attractive, good-looking, vivacious and everything that I wanted to be when I grew up.

* * *

My first visit to a French country market had me really worried. I followed Claire from stall to stall and wondered nervously why she was arguing with all of them. First the fishmonger. The piece of fish was examined, turned over, shouted over, gesticulated over.

'*Alors!*'

'*Mais non!*'

'*Impossible!*'

'*Mais, madame!*'

'*Mais, monsieur!*'

Then sudden smiles, wrapping up of produce …

'*Merci, monsieur.*'

'*Au revoir, madame, et merci!*'

'*A demain!*'

And so on to the fruiterer and the same performance over a bunch of grapes. On our way home Claire explained that this was the custom. You argued over the price, the produce and then reached an amicable conclusion and looked forward to the next day's bargaining. She assured me that her relationship with the local tradesmen was excellent.

My education was progressing rapidly.

* * *

How can I describe my first sight of Paris? It wasn't the Eiffel Tower, or Notre Dame or the Arc de Triomphe that I remember. All those and many other sights I came to appreciate on subsequent visits. For me it was the cafés that made such an impression. I had never seen outdoor cafés; people sitting at little tables spread over the pavement, sipping coffee, drinking beer and wine and watching the world go by. And it was the smell of coffee and patisserie, I can't quite define it, but it comes back every time I see tables and chairs on a pavement on a warm summer's day, anywhere.

One day Uncle Vivid took us to a posh restaurant. For him and Claire it must have been an exhilarating experience too: to be free to sit in such elegant surroundings, after all those years in hiding. Prepared to try anything new, I had *moules marinières*, in great silvered buckets. Paris was a celebration of food and freedom.

I was so amazed by all I saw, touched, tasted, smelt and felt that I had no space for envy. This was an exotic lifestyle beyond anything I could have imagined. I had read about affluence in books, usually depicting courtly life in the nineteenth century, but that wasn't the same as experiencing it at first hand. But behind the glamour and the money there was a sad tale.

We had not been long in my aunt and uncle's house before we became aware of the fraught atmosphere and a battle of wills between the two of them. The reason for this was then and is still now risible. They could not agree on whether the new cutlery they were ordering should be silver or silvered. This dilemma caused venomous exchanges, overheard from behind the closed doors of their bedroom and in public at the dining table. What amazed me most was the use of the endearment 'chérie', spat out at regular intervals. I promised myself there and then that I would never use 'darling' or any other term of affection in hate or even casually.

It wasn't until I was a little older that Ruth told me the full story behind the animosity in that beautiful chateau. Vivid had always been a womaniser but in Montmorency he excelled himself. He had a permanent mistress whom he set up in her own house in the village. She called herself Madame Levy. So for the village community there were two Madame Levys. Now this was France and having a mistress was not uncommon. But Claire was not French, and the daily humiliation must have been dreadful for her. One incident that happened while we were there was when the baker told her that the birthday cake monsieur had ordered for her was ready. Claire rushed from the shop in tears. The cake was for the other Madame Levy.

Uncle Vivid was always working in his office so apart from mealtimes and the visit to Paris we saw little of him. My memory is of a slight, energetic man with dark hair, beginning to recede, and large glasses, which reflected the outside world and hid his eyes.

One can never know the truth underlying other people's relationships, and there may have been reasons for my uncle to behave as he did. But Claire, belying her outward appearance, was not a sophisticated woman. She was a simple, warm-hearted and vulnerable person. Vivid clearly needed something more. Of course to me, then, the prevailing unhappiness was like a mysterious vapour that drifted in and out and I was having too much excitement of my own to be either curious or concerned.

One instance of my own parents' behaviour puzzled me then and still puzzles me now. The four of us made one trip into Paris on our own, and Fred bought Ruth a small bottle of French scent.

'Don't mention this to the others,' I was told. 'It's our little secret.'

I knew that all our expenses for this trip were paid for by my aunt and uncle. Why did my parents not want them to know that Fred had a little cash to spend, enough for this romantic gesture?

And so our brief mirage came to an end. On the last evening there was a soirée held in our honour. After dinner we gathered in the drawing-room; Tommy and I were allowed to stay up, a privilege I soon regretted. To my dismay I was called on to play 'Fur Elise' (that was as far as I'd got in my piano lessons). I fervently wished for a miracle to help me avoid this potential disaster and the concerned look on both my parents' faces didn't fill me with confidence.

'Come on, Renée. We'd love to hear you.'

'*Joue, petite, joue!*'

'*Courage, chérie!*'

Encouragement came from all sides. I had to play. Miraculously I got through it without mishap, even the long run at the end, which I normally stumbled over. As I played the last note, through the polite applause I heard the distinct, very audible sigh of relief from my father at the back of the room.

Next day we were on the ferry to Dover and home. I stood on the deck watching the slipstream foaming and sending a misty spray upwards. My thoughts reflected the confusion of the churning water around the boat. So many impressions, too much to digest so soon. But one thought dominated all the others. Being rich, having everything one needs and much, much more doesn't ensure happiness. We didn't have much in the way of material goods, but we were very rich in our love for each other.

Later that day I misbehaved, I can't remember how, but I was roundly told off. I tearfully wished I was back in France, amongst people who really appreciated me, and away from my unreasonable parents!

It was to be six years before I saw Paris again. I was 17 and it was my first trip away on my own. My parents saw me on to the boat train at Victoria, shouting instructions up through the smoke and above the hissing of steam.

'Don't talk to strangers!'

'Don't forget to eat your sandwiches.'

'Be nice to Claire.' (As if I wouldn't!)

'Have you got something to read on the journey?'

Read? If my mother had had any idea of the adventures I had on my journeys to and from Paris she would never have let me go.

On this trip I was joined by four young Spaniards shortly after the train pulled out of the station. They spent the entire time to Paris persuading me to cancel my plans and go on with them to Spain. Impossible though this was, they were good-looking, with their dark curly hair and dancing brown eyes and high spirits, and for one mad moment I thought it would be exciting, cutting all ties, total freedom. And I was flattered; I was still at school and knew no boys at home. Tommy's friends were 14, and much too young.

Tante Claire was at the Garde du Nord to meet me. Her circumstances had greatly changed. She and Vivid had divorced. He remained in Montmorency and had married his mistress. Claire lived in a small apartment off the Champs-Elysées. She was very unhappy. Divorce in the early fifties was not so common and still carried a stigma and though she had friends, she was lonely. Maggy and Michelle had prospered professionally, working for the French Tourist Board as specially picked hostesses at the key entrance points to the city, such as Charles de Gaulle airport and the main stations. They easily fulfilled the criteria of good looks, charm and three fluent languages. One day a handsome young American arrived in Paris. Maggy was on duty.

'Hi! Can you organise a hotel for me?'

She did more than that for him, inviting him back to her flat. They were married shortly afterwards in Montmorency. Vivid's new wife acted as hostess. Claire was not invited. It was something Ruth never forgave her niece for, although, with typical generosity, she often excused both of Claire's daughters for their callous treatment of their mother.

'Those girls didn't have a normal adolescence. They went through hell during the war, you have to understand why they turned out the way they have.'

Maggy's husband was a successful LA lawyer and soon after they had left for California Michelle decided to follow, taking her little daughter Cathy with her. So Claire was left alone. I hope she was glad to have my company and I certainly had a good time with her. She showed me Paris, my Paris, full of romance, drama and ghosts. It was a cold, windy January day when we took the bus to Montmartre. Suddenly the clouds parted and for a brief moment the wintry sun bathed the Sacre Coeur in an ethereal light. The great white church on the hill stood lit in a bright halo of sunshine. That was a theatrical moment. Then the climb up the many steps to Montmartre. The square was deserted, windswept, with paper blowing in a slow dance from corner to corner. And there were the spirits of Modigliani, Picasso, Cezanne and Toulouse Lautrec, strolling with their beautiful young mistresses and models, sitting at the cafés, drinking absinthe, calling down from the shuttered windows … I was transported to another time, remembering all I had read about the painters and poets who had lived and worked there. How glad I am that that was my first glimpse of

Montmartre. On subsequent visits, in the summer, the square was packed with souvenir stalls, tourists and American accents. No room for my 'ghosts'.

Later we were sipping our very welcome hot chocolate in a warm café on the Boulevard Saint Germain. Here I was dreamily accompanied by the spirits of Simone de Beauvoir, Sartre, Cocteau and the singer Juliette Gréco, dressed all in black, when the waiter brought a note over from the only other customers, a group of students. It was for me. I read it but couldn't understand some of the French.

'Here, Tante Claire, can you read this. I don't know what it says.'

My aunt read the note, then threw back her head and laughed out loud.

'It says "Get rid of the old bag and join us!"'

That was a good day.

Claire would visit us in Wanstead several times in those years between 1946 and 1953; always generous, affectionate and sad. She was with us on the first New Year after her divorce and as midnight approached she rushed out of the small celebration we were having in floods of tears. To my shame, I felt uncomfortable and embarrassed at this show of emotion.

It was during my last visit to her in 1954 that Claire found the lump. She came out of her tiny bathroom, her face white and drawn. Suddenly she looked old.

'Renée, I think I've got a lump in my breast. Will you go to the doctor with me?'

They suspected cancer. I went home sick at heart with the knowledge that I might not see Claire again and that I'd have to

117

tell Ruth that her sister might have cancer. The confirmation of the diagnosis came shortly after I'd returned. Ruth immediately travelled to Paris to be with her through the operation and treatment.

Claire seemed to make a good recovery at the time but the cancer had spread to her spine. In April 1956, three weeks after Ruth had organised and celebrated my wedding, with how heavy a heart at what was to come I can only imagine, she returned to Paris. Claire knew she was dying and had decided to go to America to be with her children and granddaughter. Ruth had come to help her close the flat and pack all her belongings.

Fred, true to his habit of a letter a day, informs her of all our domestic trivia, with only one mention of the sad situation:

'*Tell Claire that the Americans have better methods to treat her spine and give her my love.*' It is Tommy's scrawled postscript that makes the only reference to how Ruth must have been feeling.

'*Dear Mummy, we are all right here. I hope you are not too miserable in Paris. Hoping to see you soon. Love Tom.*'

Ruth saw her sister off at the airport knowing that she would not see her again. Claire was heavily drugged to endure the long flight and to enable her to walk at the other end, so as to avoid any problem with immigration. She died three weeks after her arrival.

Vivid died two months later. The pathologist could find no physical cause of death.

9

Leni

My aunt Leni was very different from Ruth and Claire. The second oldest, she was, outwardly at least, less feminine than her sisters. Tall, slim, athletically built, she had almost African features, with her short crinkly hair and full lips. As a child my initial impression was that of a bossy person. She seemed always to know what was best for all of us.

'Ruthimaus, you must do this.'

'Of course, Lenimaus.'

'Renée, Tommy, what are you up to?'

In unison, 'Nothing, Tante Leni!'

I hasten on to mitigate this image. Underneath the brusque exterior was a good-hearted woman, perhaps not as confident as she would want the world to believe, for whom I developed the greatest respect and admiration.

I knew Leni far less well than Claire. I didn't go to her home in Israel during her lifetime and her visits to us were rare. She also shared our bedroom, Tommy once more being banished to the camp bed. And, as with Claire, I would secretly watch her get ready for bed. She had none of the finery of her older sister, rather scorning any outward show or adornment. She always wore tailored slacks, shirts and sweaters. She would have loved the

119

modern day freedom of jeans and T-shirts. It was her body that fascinated me, the small high breasts and flat stomach, so youthful, not at all what I thought a woman in her fifties should look like.

Leni was also a lifelong chain smoker. The continuous wafts of smoke and the surrounding aroma gave her an air of sophistication that I greatly admired. I was also curious about the fact that she had only one child (my cousin Hannelore is nine years older than me). All the children that I knew had siblings.

'Well,' she would explain, with the inevitable cigarette dangling in brown stained fingers, 'You see, when we were young the world was such a bad place we didn't think it was right to bring any more children into it.'

Even then, aged eleven, I could not accept this as a reason. Surely children would help make the world a better place for the next generation. And I was quite sorry for Hannelore, and wondered what it had been like for her as an only child.

Born in 1897, Leni was eight years older than Ruth. Edith, the sister who disappeared, was born in the intervening years. Where Claire, the first child, the pretty one, was fussed over, petted and spoilt, Leni, not so pretty, not made much fuss of, soon learned to compensate by using her brain. Hardworking, she did well at school and became the assistant director in a private bank, Schindler's, earning a good salary – quite an achievement for a young woman at that time.

She met and married Fritz Weill (brother to Kurt) in 1924. Aged 17, he was conscripted from school to serve as a medical orderly in the First World War. When peace came the government offered young men in this field of work 'fast track' training, that is, no breaks in the year, so when he got married to Leni, aged 24, he already had his doctorate. After he had set up in practice my mother worked for him as his assistant for a while. I have touched on the reasons for her leaving (his more than brotherly-in-law attentions) in Ruth's story.

In the early years of their marriage Leni and Fritz had a country cottage 'Klein Steinberg', 17 kilometres east of Leipzig, often mentioned by Ruth with nostalgia and affection, where family and friends gathered at weekends and for holidays. It was here that Ruth's friendship with Kurt Weill began.

In 1936 Leni and Fritz, with their little daughter Hannelore, now nine years old, decided to emigrate to Palestine. There were several reasons for this. Firstly, his parents and sister were already there. Secondly, up to 1935 the British mandate had welcomed doctors from other countries to practise in Palestine, recognising their foreign qualifications. All this was about to change. After 31 December 1936 all immigrating doctors had to study again, as Fred did in the UK. But the most pressing reason was the declaration that from 1936 Jewish doctors were not allowed to practise privately in Germany. So, to beat all the deadlines they travelled to Palestine, staying initially with his family in Jerusalem. Leni had always wanted to live by the sea, and whilst still in Germany had bought a plot of land on the northern coast of what was then Palestine, in a place called Naharya. They were among the first hundred pioneers. It was a large area of sand dunes with a derelict hotel once used by the British. Leni and Fritz built a makeshift bungalow. This remained at the bottom of their garden when they eventually built their house and became my parents' little home on their annual visits. Here Leni began what was largely to be her life's work. Together with the others who joined, Arabs and Jews, they cleared the rocks and stones and worked the land, planting the orange and lemon trees that line the roads, and built a community. It was a hard life but Hannelore remembers it as a great adventure. Leni's routine never varied. She was up at 5 a.m. and went to bed after midnight. She swam two or three times a day, far out to sea. She cultivated her own two acres, growing vegetables and grapes. During the war and after, she rented rooms in the house often sleeping in the bathtub to ensure everyone else had a bed. She cooked for the entire household.

Leni was a true socialist in that she practised what she preached. To her it was what a person did that mattered, not who they were. Typically, when she became ill towards the end of her life, she insisted on being in a public ward.

'But, Leni,' urged her friends and her daughter, 'this was your husband's hospital. You should use the privileges that are yours.'

'No. If it's good enough for other women, it's good enough for me!'

Meanwhile, as Leni helped to make the desert fertile and bloom, Fritz, not so practical with his hands, but gifted in languages, set about learning Arabic. Then he bought a horse. For the next eleven years he rode to all the neighbouring Arab villages administering to their medical needs, delivering babies and conducting a wide spread 'general practice'. He was paid in kind: vegetables, butter, lamb.

On October 1947 the British government decided to end their unpopular mandate, now rejected by almost all the population of Palestine, though for contradictory reasons. On 20 November the General Assembly of the United Nations, after intensive discussions and some 'arm twisting' by the United States, endorsed the Jewish state and voted in favour of partition, 33 for, 13 against, including all the 11 Muslim states, and 10 abstentions, including Britain.

Within hours of the United Nations vote, Naharya was

surrounded by hostile Arabs, including men from the surrounding states such as Syria, and completely cut off.

Conor Cruise O'Brien, diplomat and journalist, and himself a member of the United Nations, describes in his book *The Siege*, how the British government reacted to the General Assembly recommendations. In December they made it known that they would not withdraw immediately but would continue to rule in Palestine for the five months until 15 May, when they would declare the mandate at an end, but in the meantime they would make no attempt to facilitate partition.

In April, Leni and Fritz could not get to Hannelore's wedding in Haifa because of the siege and spent the day sitting on the beach looking longingly and in vain for a boat or any means to get to their only daughter's wedding just a few miles down the coast.

The five terminal months of the mandate gave the Arab states time to rearm with British cooperation, and when fighting broke out immediately after the United Nations' vote between Arabs and Jews, the British forces did not intervene. Indeed they went further: they attempted to influence the outcome by confiscating Jewish arms wherever they found them.

Attacks by Arabs against Jews and reprisals against Arabs with the continuous propaganda of fear resulted in approximately 300,000 Palestinian Arabs fleeing their home, seeking temporary sanctuary in neighbouring countries, whose broadcasts reassured them that they would return to their homes as soon as the Arab states had conquered the fledgling Jewish state. Amongst that number, to her dismay, were Leni's neighbours, although many of those in the surrounding villages remained.

On 14 May in Tel Aviv, Ben-Gurion, as prime minister, proclaimed the State of Israel. On the following day at 6 p.m. (11 a.m. Washington time) the British mandate expired. Eleven minutes later President Truman announced America's recognition of Israel. But this did not signal peace. Within hours of the mandate ending, five Arab states attacked Israel. Egyptian planes bombed Tel Aviv, and Ben-Gurion's first broadcast, as prime minister of Israel, was from an air raid shelter.

Like my father, Fritz had taken from Germany the necessary equipment for a small hospital. This had remained in storage, transported and housed in a 'lift' (a crate the approximate size of a shed) since their arrival in 1936. Now, in the emergency situation, Fritz set up a makeshift hospital in the derelict hotel. After five months Naharya was liberated. When the war ended in 1949 the authorities built a new hospital in Naharya where Fritz worked for the rest of his life.

*　*　*

Fritz was as congenitally unfaithful to Leni as Vivid was to Claire. But somehow he was forgiven. Leni was very much her own woman, independent before she married and that gave her great strength. His daughter, Hannelore, told me:

'He just couldn't help himself. Women threw themselves at him. He was charming, good-looking, it wasn't his fault.'

I met Fritz when they came to London when I was twelve. We took them to Hampton Court Palace and Uncle Fritz had a risqué joke for almost everything we saw, particularly the fountains. I was doubled up with laughter, I thought he was wonderful. That was the only time I saw him. He died in 1957, aged 60, of heart disease. Both Kurt and another brother died relatively young of heart attacks.

The unfaithfulness of both my uncles was for many years a mystery to me. My own father did lapse once in Germany, encouraged by Ruth's idealistic image of a modern 'free' marriage, both being unaware of how deeply damaging this would be, but as far as I know he remained faithful to Ruth after that. I had the example of steady, devoted parents, despite the occasional rows, sulks and silences. Did their strict puritanical upbringing affect the sisters? I know that Ruth was inhibited in some ways, but not in others. She quite happily walked around the house naked and we often bathed together. Major decisions were discussed in those long, hot soaks, but she would be shocked at the word 'farting', which Fred would love to tease her with, much to our delight, and sexual references were not encouraged.

Leni died in 1973, in Naharya. She had been ill for some time, a cyst growing ever bigger inside her until all her organs were affected. Ruth and Fred were with her when they tried to operate, unsuccessfully. She put great store in Fred's medical judgement and wanted him to be there. Much of her deterioration, he felt, was related to her lifelong addiction to tobacco.

Hannelore visited her every day. One day Leni asked her not to come the next day.

'Have a little time for yourself. Take a rest. I'll see you later.' And she kissed her daughter goodbye. The following day Leni pulled out all the tubes that were keeping her alive and passed away peacefully.

*   *   *

Naharya is now a thriving seaside town with its avenues of trees, irrigated by streams with little bridges for pedestrians. On the very edge of the glimmering sea there is a cemetery. There you will find the headstone of Leni and Fritz Weill. At the side of the grave there is a small pile of stones. Underneath, buried in the sand, are the ashes of Ruth and Fred. So the sisters remain together.

The last word about the three sisters is a happy one, for indeed the little time we had together was special. How often have I thought that if there had been no war what a rich family life Tommy and I might have had, with grandparents, aunts, uncles and cousins.

There is one endearing, even hilarious memory I have above all others, that, to me, epitomises the *esprit* between the three sisters. The year was 1949 and, on a rare occasion, both Claire and Leni had come to stay in our new home in Wanstead. At the time Tennessee Williams' latest play *A Streetcar Named Desire* was playing at the Aldwych theatre. The sisters planned to see the play and, knowing my passion for the theatre, they decided to take me with them. However, because of the adult content of the drama there was an age limit, 18 and over only. I was a gawky, pigtailed, spotty and by today's standards *very* young, 14-year-old. Undeterred, Leni bought four tickets. The great day arrived and I remember the howls of laughter as my mother and my two aunts produced stockings, high heels and a selection of their clothes. They were like three young girls planning an escapade together. They dressed me in whatever fitted best and made me practise walking in the unaccustomed shoes, then sat me down in front of Ruth's secondhand utility dressing-table and buzzed around with eye-shadow, mascara, lipstick, rouge. They discussed hair styles – not much choice with my two thin plaits – and in the end they put my hair up in a top knot.

Feeling like a princess and looking well over 18, I accompanied the three of them to the theatre. I didn't understand the delicate allusion to homosexuality of course, but I was left with a powerful impression of Blanche DuBois' vulnerability as portrayed by Vivien Leigh. Given the ethos of the time, how many mothers and aunts would have taken a teenager to such an adult play?

In the future Claire would take me to see the best of Paris theatre at the Theatre National and The Comedie Français and Ruth continued my education at home but it was this one occasion, their sense of fun, of adventure, which gave me an insight into what it must have been like for Claire, Leni, Edith and Ruth growing up together in Leipzig.

10

Home!

Even after Fred had passed his exams my parents continued to struggle to make ends meet in Kilburn. His prediction that it would be hard to find a position as a surgeon was proved right. He set up in private practice with a room in Harley Street, but the income from this was minimal, only just covering the rent there. He had two or three patients, people who remembered him from the north; Mrs Wigglesworth's son, Walter, from Marple was one. But my father didn't have the connections and 'old boy' network necessary to establish himself. Locum jobs and Ruth's continuing efforts kept us afloat in what seemed like a never-ending sea of insecurity. Fred worked for a while at Stoke Mandeville hospital, where they made and fitted artificial limbs, commuting home at weekends; his wartime experience with injured soldiers was useful. After that he took any other locum job that came along, often to far flung regions of London. One was in Tooting, as visiting doctor to a mental institution, two or three times a week. Another, as emergency doctor to a hospital in Lewisham, which meant that he could be called out at any time, day or night. All this entailed speedy travel and it quickly became apparent that he needed a car. We had no money, so Ruth asked her sister Leni in Israel for a loan of £300. Ruth was always very proud and hated to ask for favours, even from her sister, and there was much soul-searching and deliberation before the request was made but as Fred said, 'Who else can we ask? We have no choice.'

Leni, who was not short of money, gladly gave us the £300, which Ruth and Fred assiduously repaid as soon as they were able to in spite of her protests to 'forget it'. We bought one of the first new Austins that broke the black or grey tradition; it was a delicate pale blue and we were all immensely proud of it.

The car now became useful for job hunting. Tommy and I remember sitting outside a surgery in south London for what seemed hours, bored, hungry and impatient while our father had an interview. He didn't get that position. I don't know how many such disappointments he went through, but we were old enough now to understand the stress they were under. After the tensions of separation and then the exams, this was their low point, the nearest they came to losing hope.

But always present was the knowledge of what might have been, and how blessed we were to be alive and have each other. We had a visitor during this time who brought us a painful reminder of this fact. Ilse Frankenthall was the widow of Fred's former chief, Ludwig Frankenthall, at the Jewish hospital in Leipzig. We had never seen anyone so wasted and ashen-faced. My brother and I were shocked by her appearance. She looked like a walking corpse. Ruth told me her story after she had left us. Together with her husband and two children she was taken to Auschwitz. He was ordered to castrate prisoners or they would kill his children. He refused. They killed him and the two children. She survived and was working in a factory making light bulbs. She had been a concert pianist. I remember how she played Chopin for us on my old piano and what she said. 'Now my life is in my hands, it's in the hands.'

Then, early in 1949, Fred found an advertisement in the *British*

Medical Journal for an assistant in a practice in the East End of London. A junior partnership would follow after a three month trial period. Fred drove to Leytonstone for an interview with a Dr Kearney. He was immediately offered the job. Finally our luck had changed and we were jubilant.

The post was conditional on our moving into the district as soon as possible. With much excitement we began to plan our new life; should we buy or rent a house?

'Buy, definitely!' said Ruth and Fred, in one breath. Long-term commitment and security were now within reach.

So far so good! Fred started work in Leytonstone immediately while we were still living in Kilburn, commuting early in the morning and returning after the evening surgery.

It soon became apparent that the Kearneys (and Ruth always insisted that it was Mrs Kearney's plan) wanted us to buy a house in Leytonstone near the surgery. It would obviously make her husband's life easier if the assistant lived next to the job.

Leytonstone then was a rundown, poor district with mainly terraced working men's cottages with front doors opening straight on to the pavement. Even in our shabby rented Kilburn house we had a patch of garden in the front and a larger one in the back. We had a gate and a fence! Ruth took one look at Leytonstone, summed it up as a working-class area, and was not impressed. This was not what she had been waiting for all these years. At the same time she ascertained that Dr and Mrs Kearney lived in the leafy suburb of Wanstead, just 15 minutes' drive from the surgery, with its *bijou* cinema, village atmosphere and semi and detached houses with large gardens. Thus, the search for a house in Wanstead, which we could afford, began.

The first time Tommy and I were taken to view 74 Overton Drive, Wanstead, we were in a state of high excitement and anticipation. Nothing could have prepared us for the thrill we felt when we saw the place. At 11 and 14 we were too young and inexperienced – after all we had never had a home of our own – to see the poor state of repair the house was in (suspected bomb damage), nor did the overgrown garden, given over to potatoes during the war, bother us. I loved the enormous cherry tree in the back garden, which was just beginning to show the promised profusion of white blossom, and which in another week would resemble the aftermath of a snow storm. I was enchanted by it all: the apples and pears at the bottom of the garden, a little orchard where chickens would soon roost; the knowledge that I would have my own room for the first time; the space, the privacy, the sense of our own territory – all these emotions made that first visit so memorable. I grew to love the open aspect facing the house, the lake opposite with the surrounding golf course, but at that moment this was outside the cocoon of the property, which enfolded me in warmth and security, and therefore of less interest. But for Ruth and Fred the view clinched the deal! And they could just afford it. The house cost £3,000 and, with no cash available, to procure the 100 per cent loan needed, Fred took out a life insurance policy for that sum as a guarantee.

We moved in on 1 April 1949 with our few possessions and the wonderment of ownership that I have never lost.

It only took a few weeks of our new life in Wanstead before certain rumours began to reach Fred's ears. Dr Kearney was said to be a heavy drinker. Even more disturbing, he had had three assistants before Fred, luring them into the area and then sacking them before the three months' trial period was over. As this time was now coming to an end Fred approached Dr Kearney with the request to formalise the agreement, which would make him a junior partner in the practice. Dr Kearney refused.

'Don't worry,' said Ruth. 'You've got an agreement. He can't do anything to you.'

Fred sat silent.

'Fred?' My mother's voice began to rise several decibels. 'You did sign an agreement with him?'

'We spoke. It was between gentlemen.'

A combination of expletives in German and English rained down like a hailstorm. Suffice it to say that there was nowhere in our spacious house to seek shelter.

'You will go now, to his house, and get him to sign that you will be a partner.'

'He *will* honour it. We have a gentlemen's agreement!' persisted my ever-trusting father.

'Like hell he will! First thing tomorrow before surgery you get him to put his signature. On the back of an envelope, anything! Our whole future depends on this! We have a house to pay for!'

Fred knew she was right. But he hated conflict, and, seeing his crestfallen face, I understood how reluctant he was to act. However, he did confront Dr Kearney on the next day only to be met by further procrastination. For my parents the partnership was crucial, not only for the considerable rise in salary to pay the mortgage, but also without that security we could lose everything. Ruth once told me that Fred had reached such a low ebb of despair that he had even contemplated suicide so that we would get his life insurance, enough to give us the house, a roof over our heads. I believe it was more of a dramatic gesture, driven by feelings of guilt. He must have been aware that suicide would negate the insurance.

Ruth's instinct, that it was Mrs Kearney, somewhat younger than her husband, who masterminded the sabotaging of partnerships and the pressure for us to live in Leytonstone, was probably correct. The couples never socialised but Fred got to know Dr Kearney well enough to discern that he may have been unhappy at home. Fred told Tommy that one evening, surgery being over, Fred was on his way out when he noticed Dr Kearney's door was ajar and he'd not gone home. Looking in to say goodnight he found him sitting at his desk, head in hands.

'Everything OK? You going home?' my father inquired.

'I'd rather stay here than go home,' was the response.

Fred sensed that Dr Kearney was well meaning but ineffective, perhaps willing to take the road of least resistance.

The threat of legal action (we had contacted a lawyer recommended by Walter Wigglesworth) finally ended the saga. The lawyer assured my parents that even if they had had a letter, it would not have been worth the paper it was written on. A legal document was drawn up and Fred became the junior partner in the practice.

Six months later Dr Kearney died of a heart attack and my father took over the whole practice and ran it alone until he retired in 1973.

And so we settled down to normal family life, with its highs and lows, endless conflicts and much happiness. At last Ruth was able to relax. She got help in the house and she could indulge her love of good quality clothes and expensive make-up. She taught me the importance of skincare, swearing that Helena Rubinstein was the only make worth considering, and despairing when I defiantly bought pots of cold cream.

Did Fred mind giving up surgery, a skill at which he excelled? I often asked him and he always denied that it mattered to him, saying that a good surgeon is not an old surgeon. Any regrets he may have had he kept well hidden and I chose to believe him.

His major interest now lay in making the house our own. This was the great DIY era, and Fred flourished, all his creative energy now redirected into designing, planning and searching for the right products. They spent years happily changing everything to their liking, although there were the occasional arguments. I remember one in particular about lavatory seats. Should the one in the outside toilet be as expensive as the posh one in the bathroom? She said, 'Yes.' He said, 'No.' She won!

Tommy and I were involved, reluctantly or otherwise, whenever possible. While I was still at school I spent several weekends with Fred decorating his very functional, rather depressing surgery on Leytonstone High Road. Driving to the surgery with him I was fascinated by the houses being demolished all around. This was the time of the big post-war building programme, when the terraces were being replaced by tower blocks. Whole communities, with their local store and pub, were disbanded and many of Fred's patients were rehoused. He believed that their conditions would be greatly improved with modern facilities. But I was moved and strangely saddened to see the two-up, two-down homes, open to the elements like doll's houses, with some walls already gone, others still displaying the torn wallpaper that someone had chosen with care.

I don't know who chose the colour scheme for the surgery or whether it was an NHS directive to use up surplus paint, but I remember painting pale blue walls and all the woodwork a dark maroon. These were rare opportunities to be alone with my father and enjoy his company. We listened to music on the wireless and talked and I knew he appreciated my help.

I disagreed with most of their decisions, partly because I was a rebellious, morose teenager, but also I realise now that I had a burgeoning sense of my own style. My inherent attraction to objects from the past began to develop. There was a Victorian desk left in Fred's surgery quite at odds with the ugly concrete block that housed it. My parents hated this desk and vowed to dispose of it as soon as possible. Aged 15, I begged them to keep it for when I had my own home. I am sitting at it now. While exploring in an old warehouse I found and then persuaded them to buy a Queen Anne inlaid marquetry bureau with matching chair (now in Mississippi with my brother), and the pretty antique table they had in the window of their bedroom. There wasn't much else in the house that I liked. Ruth would ask, 'What d'you think of this?' or 'Do you like that?' And I would shrug, dismissively. 'It's not really my taste.'

Now I look around my home and see all the things I brought with me when we cleared the house and wish that she could see that I have them. I think of her every time I look at them, with love and also shame that I was so ungracious. I did so like to shock her. When I eventually had a home of my own I collected old chamber pots. Ruth was horrified when I filled them with fruit and nuts for Christmas!

It was the changes in the garden that I regretted the most. I would come home in the late afternoon from school (I remained at Parliament Hill School in Highgate so had a long journey every day) to find some new terrible act had been committed. First, the great cherry tree, of superb blossom but poor fruit, came down to be replaced by a small morello cherry tree. For the next 50 years this tree would be the bane of our lives. Every spring it had to be covered with a net to protect the cherries from the birds; this never worked, they ate their fill! In the autumn the net would have to be removed and untangled! Was the little fruit we harvested worth all that?

Then the orchard at the back of the garden, where the chickens pecked and rambled free, was decimated, leaving only one apple tree, and two garages were erected. The chickens were confined to cages. The lawn laid in the early fifties, permanently scarred by the first pair in a long line of cocker spaniel bitches peeing on it, was largely replaced by a swimming pool in the sixties, prescribed by consultants to help Ruth's rheumatic pains. The pool became an endless source of fun for family, neighbours and friends. Apart from the early years when my children were toddlers; trying to prevent them falling in made every visit a nightmare! My mother liked nothing better than to have us all gathered in the garden, serving us iced coffee heaped with whipped cream, and home-made cake.

There were, however, some changes that I was delighted with. One was my bedroom. In 1949, shortly after we'd moved in Ruth wrote:

You have a very nice big room facing the garden and so far you have not got any nice furniture. We hope to be able in not too long a time to furnish your room as a bed-sitting room in which you can receive your friends and I hope it will be so nice (you will choose it yourself) that it will be the first room to start your married life with one day, if it should be necessary.

The promised refurbishing came sooner than expected. A few months later I contracted pneumonia and was in Wanstead hospital for ten days, enough time for my parents to be able to surprise me on my return. What excitement and how spoilt I felt on seeing what they had achieved. I now was the proud possessor of a built-in wardrobe, shelves for my books, incorporating a little desk and more cupboard space underneath. I still have the thirties dressing-table they had placed by the window. And though I did not start my married life there, my mother's prediction was almost true. I did live there briefly as a married woman and with a baby when my husband's work brought us back to London, from Nottingham.

My children loved the regular Sundays we spent in Wanstead. To this day they talk affectionately about the Wiener schnitzel for lunch with tiny tinned potatoes and carrots, the height of luxury as far as they were concerned. And then there were the pears! They became a family joke. Fred grew espalier pears along the fence down one side of the garden, approximately 75 feet, producing an abundance of large, hard and inedible pears. Every autumn he would hurry home from the surgery and visits to peel, core, stew and freeze pears in dozens of containers carefully labelled. Over Sunday lunch, like a well-rehearsed sketch, came the inevitable exchange:

'What's for pudding?'

'Guess!'

'What are we having *with* the pears?'

'Ice cream.' The accompaniment was the only variable, cream or custard were other possibilities!

'When d'you think I picked these pears?' Fred would ask, the corners of his mouth twitching.

We would feign interest or curiosity. Fred would then proudly announce the vintage – which could be anything up to three years – of the rather tasteless compote and he would grin, regardless of whether we dutifully acted out our amazement or failed to conceal our disgust.

* * *

How different would our lives have been if there had been no Hitler, no war?

'The only favour Hitler did us was to send us to England,' Ruth and Fred always insisted. Ruth especially never felt totally at ease in Germany, aware of the overt racism in a way that Fred, with his non-Jewish boyhood friends and his football and music associates, did not feel.

As a teenager I was unaware of any anti-Semitism in this country and shortly after we moved to Wanstead I casually suggested to Fred:

'Why don't you join the golf club? It's a way of meeting people. You don't have far to go ... it's only over the road!' The course was opposite our house, a horseshoe bordering the lake.

My father looked at me, almost pityingly, his mouth twitching at the corners in that ironic way of his.

'Jews aren't accepted,' he replied briefly. I was shocked. All our efforts not to be Jewish, the denials, the baptisms, were in vain.

The birth of the State of Israel in 1947 became the pivot of all Ruth's hopes and fears; the safe haven for us all to go to if persecution came again, a nirvana of peace and safety. She raged and suffered with each successive war in that region, but was equally distressed at the plight of the Boat People in the eighties. She wept for all displaced and persecuted people.

In spite of their undying gratitude and respect for Winston Churchill, they voted Labour in 1945 but they never forgave Ernest Bevin, the foreign secretary, for his policy in turning survivors of the concentration camps away from the shores of Israel and forcing them into camps in Cyprus. Though genuine socialists at heart, they became staunch supporters of the Conservative party.

When I questioned why we had not gone to Israel after the war,

Fred's response was: 'Because every other road builder and farmer is a surgeon or doctor.'

And Ruth's: 'Too many Jews!' Yet she often voiced her fears for the future of that country, echoing her youthful Cassandra epithet.

Passionate as she was for the survival of Israel, an ardent supporter of the WIZO (Women's International Zionist Organisation), she nevertheless maintained her cosmopolitan values and retained an instinctive fear of being labelled. Was this another reminder of the past, never again to be part of a Jewish community? There was so much they wanted to forget, so, after the loss of their library, no books were bought, except for those for Tommy and me, and no saxophone was played. They bought a clarinet for Tommy's 13th birthday and he overheard Fred playing it, just once.

One of the effects of our escape for my brother and me was the loss of our extended family. We were so fortunate that most of our family survived, but they were scattered around the world, the US, Israel, France, South Africa, Australia. We never really knew our grandparents, and our cousins grew up, married, and had their families elsewhere.

Apart from their support for the WIZO, my parents did not seek out or subscribe to the local Jewish community. The only time we visited a synagogue was for the wedding of Ilse, our teenage babysitter from Leipzig, and Leonard. We were still living in Kilburn at the time. Tommy and I were most impressed by the ceremonial smashing of the wine glasses, but my predominant memory was of Ruth's anxiety to plait my hair in such a way that the lice I had at the time were not too visible! My first introduction to a service was in Paris when I was 17 with Aunt Claire, and I remember the beautiful singing of the cantor.

Would Ruth and Fred have stayed together if they had lived out their lives in Germany? Would they have overcome the rows and differences if they hadn't had to stand united against the outside world? Here they never made the close friends they had had, sometimes from childhood, in Germany.

'You make friends when you are young,' Ruth was fond of saying. 'Not later in life.'

Would Tommy and I have had greater independence, less interference, as we grew up? Would we have felt less Jewish if Hitler hadn't made us 'special'? Questions that have no answer, but linger, nevertheless.

Fred became increasingly derisive of all organised religions. 'A lot of hocus pocus!' And Ruth's lasting lament was 'Why do Christians hate the Jews?' She remained all her life deeply hostile to Germany and Germans. She was also antagonistic towards Poles. And yet she accepted and loved her Polish son-in-law, an acceptance that came with conditions: he had to lose his Polish name. And that is where my story started, and now I am coming to the end.

My mother lived in Wanstead for 44 years, my father for 50. They were well known locally and well liked. In the last years the chemist personally delivered medication and oxygen cylinders to the house for Ruth. As did the librarian with the latest publications when she could no longer pick them up herself.

They were a private couple, kept themselves to themselves. They would exchange gardening gossip with their neighbours and occasionally share a cup of tea, but never became intimate and always remained on formal name terms. In the sixties Fred treated one of our neighbours, Mr Ellis, privately. He arranged for a nurse to visit. When a black nurse arrived at the house Mr Ellis sent her away.

'I don't want "that sort" nursing me!' he told my father.

'Then you will have to find yourself another doctor, Mr Ellis. Either she remains or I go.'

The nurse remained and was duly much appreciated by both Mr and Mrs Ellis.

True to the period, Ruth took care to preserve the dignified image of the local doctor. In the midst of a DIY job or gardening, if Fred needed to go to the hardware store for materials or equipment, she made sure he would always change into a jacket and tie.

Everyone who met them loved Ruth and Fred. They enjoyed her warm hospitality and her genuine interest in their lives. She was a true listener. They enjoyed Fred's wry sense of humour, his ability to poke fun without malice and his tolerance for the friends who said, 'Fred, I know I shouldn't ask this over dinner, but I've had this pain/ache/disorder...'

When I meet old friends now they remind me of the good times they had in Wanstead. I must have taken everyone I knew to visit over the years and they all went back again, not necessarily with me.

Although my parents' relationship was often fraught it was built and sustained on the rock of survival. Without their courage and persistence I would not be here to tell this tale. Ruth and Fred gave me life twice over. They were, as I knew them, contentious, infuriating at times, invariably generous, both with their time and money, always loving, fun to be with, good company and for much of the time my best friends.

And so I will leave them, again at Sunday lunch, where I began, but now with more places set at the table, a family enlarged over the years, with our roots established in this country. These were the good times we will all remember.

'More pears, anyone?'

Epilogue

In October 2006, my brother and I returned to Leipzig for the first time since we fled in August 1939.

My fears of how I would feel, revisiting the places of my infancy, being in the environment where our parents had suffered so much fear and anxiety, proved to be unfounded.

The warmth and friendliness from the people we met, the acknowledgement we found in the memorials to the lost Jews of Leipzig, took away any bitterness I have felt in the past.

Our four day visit proved to be an emotional roller-coaster, full of shocks and surprises. We were shown around the Eitingon-Haus, formerly the Israelitischen hospital where Fred worked. The Star of David, removed during the Reich and Communist regimes, is now restored on the elegant façade. The cellar, where Ruth and Fred hid people on the run or returning from the camps, is still there.

At Sedanstrasse 17a, the house where Tommy and I were born (the name of the street is now different, changed during the Communist regime), we met the present caretakers, Sonja and Dieter, who were so pleased that we had come back, insisting that we had coffee with them. They showed us the stairs where Ruth had bumped her pram down to give Fred time to flee, and as we walked round the back of the building, there was the fire escape just as she had described it.

At the Jewish community offices we met Klaudia Krenn, who promptly produced all the available records of our family. We learned of what really happened to Ruth's sister, Edith. In the publication *Menschen ohne Grabstein* (People Without Graves) by Ellen Bertram, there is an entry for Edith Frankenberg. It states that Edith, born 5 April 1903, described as *Haustochter* (daughter of the house), was taken to JH (*Judenhaus*) Alexandrastrasse 46, then for hard labour until 21 January 1942 when she was deported to Riga concentration camp. There the trail ends, leaving many more questions unanswered.

We spent half a day at the Schulmuseum with Leona Bielitz, who opened the museum especially for us on a Sunday. Her enthusiasm for her work with the children in Leipzig was impressive. The schoolchildren's project is to commemorate all those who have no graves with large wire trees festooned with thousands of handkerchiefs, each one with a name and a date, and underneath the trees, stones, again with name, in the Jewish tradition. We left a handkerchief and a stone for Edith.

Leona took us to the site of the synagogue in central Leipzig, destroyed on 11 November 1938. This night is no longer referred to as *Kristallnacht*. On all the memorials and literature we read about '*Reichspogromnacht*'. Leona explained that since 1988 this change had happened throughout Germany, not through legislation but by natural evolution.

'It was felt that the description *Kristallnacht* was a euphemism for what happened that night.'

In a bookshop we discovered, amongst stories of survivors, a hardback, *Wir Waren Eure Nachbarn* (We Were Your Neighbours), published in 1996. In checking the index we found Bergmann, and to our amazement a page telling the story of the young surgeon and his wife with a picture of Tom and me with our nanny Ilse taken in the hospital grounds. We were delighted to find 'our' book in the other bookshops we browsed.

We found our grandparents' houses, where Ruth and Fred were brought up. The Frankenberg's residence in a grand house in fashionable Leipzig, the Bergmann's department store in a more working-class district, now identified with the Turkish community, with coffee shops and ethnic food stores where Fred's friend the butcher's son would have lived. We smiled as we remembered Ruth's occasional parting shot in an argument with Fred about the superiority of the Frankenbergs to the Bergmanns!

We had a meal in the famous student beer cellar, Auerbach Keller, where Goethe visited in 1759 and which is recorded in his *Faust*, and I wondered how often Ruth and Fred came there on a date.

On our last day, we were looking at a glass-fronted street map. 'Can I help you?'

A tall, white-haired man stood behind us. We explained, in our hesitant German, that we were looking for Markgraffenstrasse, where our grandparents had lived. He introduced himself, Dr Kari-Heinz Kraemer. In our 20 minute conversation on the pavement it turned out that he had worked in Fred's hospital when it became a women's hospital under the communists. And he had heard of our father. Since my return to London he has emailed me with information that he has found Fred's dissertation on kidney stones in children, registered in the Leipzig University medical records. I am happy that our father's achievement remains on record in the place of his birth.

As we walked by the station, across the wide open spaces, past the opera house, or from our home to the hospital, seeing the restoration to the elegant city Leipzig had been, I envisaged my mother following this path as a girl, as a young woman, taking Tommy and me for walks and I felt glad to be there.

The writing of this book was the catalyst for our visit. The awareness I found, the acknowledgement of the Holocaust, and the work to remember those who were lost, gave it, for me, a truly healing outcome.

Bibliography

Darton, Lawrence, *The Work of the Friends Committee for Refugees and Aliens 1933–50.* Issued by the Friends Committee for Refugees and Aliens, 1954.

O'Brien, Conor Cruise, *The Siege: The Saga of Israel and Zionism*, Simon & Schuster, 1988.

Read, Anthony & Fisher, David, *Kristallnacht*, Michael Joseph, London, 1989.

Smith, Michael, *Foley: The Spy Who Saved 10,000 Jews*, Politico's Publishing, London, 1999.

Weiner, Peter F., *Martin Luther, Hitler's Spiritual Ancestor*, Hutchinson & Co., London & New York, 1945.